TRANSF

To Ceri
Your commitment to Christ, to truth and to me has
been inspirational beyond words. Thank you.

Transforming Life

STUART LEES

KINGSWAY PUBLICATIONS
EASTBOURNE

First published in 1997 by Hodder & Stoughton
as *Will the Real Me Please Stand Up*
This new edition published by Kingsway 2003

ISBN 1 84291 144 9

Published by
KINGSWAY COMMUNICATIONS LTD
Lottbridge Drove, Eastbourne BN23 6NT, England.
Email: books@kingsway.co.uk

Book design and production for the publishers by
Bookprint Creative Services, P.O. Box 827, BN21 3YJ, England.
Printed in Great Britain.

Thanks

Many thanks to Darren, Gail, Jim, John and Lin for taking the time to read the draft manuscript, and for all your help and support.

Thanks also to Tim, James, Jonty and Sarah; you guys are the best!

Contents

Foreword

I remember, some years ago, hearing the Revd David Watson asking the question, 'If you are holding a full glass and someone nudges you, what spills out?' The answer is obvious: 'Whatever is in the glass!' But if we relate that to ourselves the answer is not so comfortable. If we are full of anger, resentment, arrogance or frustration, for whatever reason, when we're nudged it spills out. If we're filled to the brim with the love of Christ as Paul's letter to the Ephesians suggests we should be, it's love that will spill out.

But how do we get there? Well, that's what this book is all about. It gently helps us to unpack the past and all the ugliness inside us and, by applying the Word of God, begin to allow God to change us into his image. It's a long road, sometimes very uncomfortable, and this book will make *you* uncomfortable in order to get to the place where Jesus can set you free to become what he wants you to be.

When change is self-motivated it seldom lasts for long. I'm sure most of us have made resolutions on New Year's Eve which by the seventh of January have been broken and abandoned with a shrug of the shoulders!

This book shows us a different way – God's way – to change us from the inside as we surrender to his love. We read 'Once I am able to accept myself in the light of God's full acceptance of me, then I no longer need to analyse myself, compare myself or prove myself. I become free to serve, free to love, free to bless.' Powerful words! If every Christian took just that paragraph on board, I think revival would break out!

Thank you, Stuart, for writing this book. You have shown me that I still have such a long way to go in my quest for Christlikeness, but you have given me hope and shown me God's best for my life.

I pray for everyone who reads this book the prayer written in Chapter 5:

> . . . *Please teach me to see myself through your eyes and to know that I am immensely valuable to you, that I am secure in your love and that you have made me with gifts and talents that are able to bring glory to you. Thank you that I am your beloved child and that you are my perfect parent. Amen.*

Fiona Castle

Introduction

An elderly bishop wrote these words shortly before he died:

> When I was young and free and my imagination had no limits, I
> dreamed of changing the world. As I grew older and wiser, I dis-
> covered the world would not change, so I shortened my sights
> somewhat and decided to change only my country. But it, too,
> seemed immovable. As I grew into my twilight years, in one des-
> perate attempt I settled for changing only my family, those closest
> to me – but, alas, they would have none of it. Now, as I lie on my
> deathbed, I suddenly realise if I had only changed myself first, by
> example I would have changed my family. From their inspiration
> and encouragement, I would have then been able to better my
> country and, who knows, I may have even changed the world.

This book is about change. It is about changing the only
person you definitely have the power to influence – you! The
Spirit of God has put within each one of his people a longing
to change and become more like Christ. God is calling us to
be authentic people – the same on the inside as we are on the
outside. This is the essence of maturity, enabling us to be like
Christ at every level of our humanity so that how we live and

act comes out of a deeply transformed inner life. This is the only way to lasting and genuine maturity.

This book is the product of eight years of painful but lasting change in my own personal life. Like the bishop quoted above, I was keen to change the world but had not begun to allow God to change me at the deep places of my soul. My life was thoroughly inauthentic, but I did not know it at the time. I could do the work of ministry quite effectively but my inner life was far from Christlike! There was a large gap between 'being' and 'doing' in my life and it is this gap that reveals our immaturity. I do not write as one who has made it, but as one who has begun a journey; if my insights are helpful to you as you read then I shall be deeply satisfied. I hope that this is not a comfortable book, because change is never comfortable, but I do hope that it is a book that brings you comfort in the loving and life-giving presence of God.

Looking out over a glorious Scottish loch on a beautiful summer's day, I felt inspired by the wonder of God's creation, and yet I could not deny the deep frustration within me. 'Lord,' I cried, giving vent to my feelings, 'why are you so hard to find?'

Immediately I had the distinct sense that God was speaking to me. 'I am not hard to find, Stuart, but you find it hard to pull away from the world.' Ouch! That was not the answer I had been hoping for, but God certainly had my attention.

Over the next few minutes God spoke to me about my relationship with him. It was one of those moments in which his voice is clear and distinct, and ideas that I had been mulling over for a number of months were brought into sharp focus. He spoke to me about four areas that were fundamental to becoming the man that he had made me to be.

First he spoke of the nature of his grace. He has initiated a relationship with me, and is utterly committed to fulfilling his purposes in me. His grace at work in me is the basis of my journey towards wholeness and maturity.

Second he showed me that my ability to know him and to live in his loving grace is directly related to my own emotional wholeness. The more healthy I am emotionally, the more able I am to love and be loved and to enjoy his grace.

The third aspect of maturity he showed me that day was that I needed to pull away from the world and all its false pleasures and securities. To compromise with sin is to darken my spiritual eyes and to undermine the work that he is doing within me.

Finally he spoke to me about the need to develop spiritual disciplines that would enable me to take hold of the maturity that his grace had made available to me. The authenticity that I so longed for was not simply going to fall into my lap: it needed to be sought after, with all the energy and commitment that I had to give.

This was a profound moment for me because for the first time I saw the way in which these four aspects of the Christ-centred life fit together, and how each one is vital to the development of true Christian maturity. As God spoke to me I felt strengthened and encouraged to press on towards the goal of knowing Christ and being conformed into his image.

This book was born out of that conversation with the Lord, and is built around the same four areas. It is not intended to be exhaustive on each of the subjects covered, but I hope it will point a way forward to integrating these different aspects of our life in Christ in a way that is relevant and helpful.

The church in the West tends to prefer theological information to spiritual reality, often leaving it powerless and weak to transform the hearts as well as the heads of its people. I have no desire to compound this problem and therefore I have included some exercises at the end of each chapter, which are intended to help the reader enter into the reality of the teaching in this book.

> I keep asking that the God of our Lord Jesus Christ, the glorious Father, may give you the Spirit of wisdom and revelation, so that you may know him better. I pray also that the eyes of your heart may be enlightened in order that you may know the hope to which he has called you, the riches of his glorious inheritance in the saints and his incomparably great power for us who believe. (Ephesians 1:17–19)

Part 1

THE NEW CREATION

'Therefore, if anyone is in Christ, he is a new
creation. The old has gone, the new has come!'
(2 Corinthians 5:17)

1

Embracing the Real Self

As Richard finished speaking, the applause and the cheers were deafening. The speech had been a resounding success. They had loved his sense of humour, his anecdotes and his skilful turn of phrase. Grown men had wept with laughter and were slapping him on the back as he walked back to his seat. Richard was thrilled, but rather surprised, as his previous attempts at speaking in public had never met with this kind of response. In fact he had always thought that he was rather dry and lifeless as a speaker.

Sitting around the kitchen table, Richard and his wife Karen were talking about the contrast in his success at speaking. When he spoke at church he felt his words lacked life. Though the theory was good, his talks were rather hollow. But the speech at work made him feel alive. 'How could it be so different?' he asked.

'Maybe you are just not meant to speak about Christian things,' suggested Karen, but that could not have been right. Richard was creative, intelligent, funny and above all a gifted communicator. He felt called to teach and in the talks that he gave there were very definitely flashes of the real Richard that set people alight.

'Whenever I give a talk in church,' he said, 'I feel that I have to present as little of myself as possible in case I distract people from their focus on God. But when I spoke at work I wasn't trying to direct people to Christ, it was simply a farewell speech for a colleague.' Suddenly the problem became obvious. Richard did not understand that he had a real self through which God wanted to shine. In a mistaken attempt to honour God he was killing off those very qualities that the Lord himself had put into him. God was longing to flow through his intelligence, his humour and his gift with words, but all the time Richard was busy putting these things to death.

Until we are able to perceive and embrace the real person that God has made us to be, we will live a limited and unfulfilled Christian life. Though we may have come to know Christ and tasted the power of his love, we will feel dissatisfied and frustrated. The abundant life that is promised to us will always feel just out of reach, and we will be in danger of settling for second best. God wants you to shine with his life and love. He longs to fill every aspect of your being with his life-giving Spirit.

Everybody struggles

Every person who follows Christ struggles to become the person God made them to be. It is a lifelong journey and none of us has made it yet.

Ashley works for a marketing company. He has a 'big' character and is the life and soul of the party. He is successful at his career and has plenty of friends, but inside he feels lonely, inadequate and insignificant. He never feels that he measures up, and is driven by a need to prove himself. He is all at sea when he finds himself in a relationship that demands something deeper and more meaningful than being a 'good mate', and he longs to be free from sexual lust but does not know how. As a committed Christian he knows that there is something wrong and that the gap between what he presents on the outside and what he is on the inside is not healthy. He feels stuck in a rut and is unsure of how to change and grow.

Sandy has gone to the other extreme. She doesn't want to be noticed – in fact she can't bear anyone paying her any attention. Unlike Ashley who has learnt to present an image that demands to be noticed, Sandy has withdrawn into a private world. She is happy to remain hidden. She works as a nurse and finds meaning in being a servant of others, feeling safe in serving God from behind the scenes. The only trouble is that she struggles to know God's love or to develop relationships that are intimate, and she is beginning to binge on sweets and chocolate. She envies those who have close friends, but feels threatened by the prospect of having to be vulnerable, and so she remains in the safety of her isolation.

Richard, Ashley and Sandy are all struggling to live out of the real self. Like most of us, perhaps even all of us, they struggle to develop healthy and intimate relationships with God and with people. Feelings of insecurity and inadequacy undermine their joy and peace, and they recognise that they have habitual sins that leave them feeling guilty and condemned. They are only too aware that they are not yet all that God has made them to be, and are looking for some answers that will enable them to live in the freedom that they believe Christ won for them on the cross.

The biblical perspective

How can it be that God wants to reveal our true selves when we are so often taught to put the self to death, to deny the self or to empty the self? In order to embrace the true self we need to understand that this is a fully biblical principle and not an accommodation to the latest fad of our culture, preoccupied as it is with self-fulfilment and self-realisation.

Both the Old and the New Testament teach that each person has been made a unique individual, created in the image of God. The Hebrew word *nephesh* means 'soul' but it can also be translated 'self'. In Genesis 2:7 God breathes upon Adam and he becomes 'a living soul'. He becomes a 'self', a unique creature who is distinct in his identity from God and the other creatures around him. In the New Testament, the Greek word for 'self' is *autos* and means 'self, expressing distinction, exclusion'.[1]

Each of us is therefore a unique and distinct personality. I am a self and you are a self. The real question is what I choose to do with the 'self' that is me.

If I live apart from the life-giving presence of God, then I am a 'self-willed' person (Titus 1:7; 2 Peter 2:10). In this state I will create a persona and identity separate from God, but my identity will have no solid core. When everything is peeled away – my achievements, my relationships, my talents and my experiences – I will be left with nothing. At the very centre of myself will be a hollow core that is empty. There is no real identity or selfhood apart from God himself. He is the source of all identity, reality and substance and without his indwelling presence we are fundamentally empty.

The danger of being self-focused

We live in an age that is increasingly narcissistic and self-focused. Go to any bookshop and you will find an array of books that tell you how to 'find yourself', 'realise yourself', and become 'self-actualised'. This unhealthy love of the self is a symptom of a society whose people have turned away from God and now seek to worship themselves.

Narcissus was the character in Greek mythology who saw his reflection in the lake and fell in love with himself. He would gaze upon his reflection, infatuated. Finally he leant down to kiss himself, only to fall into the lake and drown.

The symbolism of the myth is unmistakable. The more infatuated we are with ourselves, the more in danger we are of losing ourselves. This is true at both a spiritual and a psychological level. Spiritually we are dead until we receive the life of Christ within us. Just as a human egg has no life in itself until fused with the sperm, so we are incomplete until we are filled with God's presence. We can only receive this life as we look up and away from ourselves to Christ. If we are to grow at a psychological level we must learn to tear our eyes away from our own selves and break our introspective thinking. We cannot grow by ourselves, we are called into maturity through that which is outside of our own personhood. We can never find ourselves because at the end of our search is an empty self devoid of Christ. Introspection destroys us at both a spiritual and a psychological level.

United with God

When we turn to God and willingly give our 'self' to him, then he comes to indwell us. As we give to him the old self with all its twisted desires, attitudes and emptiness, the Holy Spirit enters into the deepest part of our nature and begins to fill every aspect of our being. He creates a new, real and true 'self'.

> Jesus then said to his disciples: 'If any one wishes to be a follower of mine, he must leave self behind; he must take up his cross and come with me. Whoever cares for his own safety is lost; *but if a man will let himself be lost for my sake, he will find his true self.* What will a man gain by winning the whole world at the cost of his true self? Or what can he give that will buy that self back?' (Matthew 16:24–26 NEB, italics mine)

It is only as we are prepared to leave behind the old self, the rebellious self-seeking and sinful old self, that we will be able to find that we are given a new self, a new identity that is born of the Spirit. As we live according to the ways of the Spirit and as we collaborate with the will and purpose of God, his life radiates through our entire being, causing the real self to be made manifest. Every choice we make will lead us deeper into the new reality of the self in union with God, or will sabotage the redeeming work of the Spirit within us.

> We must therefore open every door of our being to this presence, to our God. It is then that we are healed in spirit, in intellect and will, and in our intuitive imaginative and sensory faculties. Christ's aim is to fill the whole life of the believer. That is what conversion is – the ongoing process of being filled with Christ. The Holy Spirit truly present and operative in the human spirit is capable of resurrecting every faculty of man.[2]

This work of the Spirit is like the restoration work that is done when a valuable old painting is found in a dusty attic. The restorer lovingly and painstakingly washes and cleans the canvas. Under his expert eye the shades and hues of the original colours are revealed and the painting once more displays the brilliance and creativity of the artist. We are God's workmanship, and through his redeeming and healing work in us, he will once again display his life, love and power in every man and woman who will die to the old self and live to the new.

Killing off the real self

It was not easy for Richard to embrace the real self because he had learned, like so many of us, to kill it off. In doing so he was putting himself to death. He had been taught to apply the words of John the Baptist to his own character: 'He must become greater and I must become less' (John 3:30).

With sincere intentions many who love Christ pray those same words for themselves, and in so doing leave themselves damaged, crippled and out of touch with the real self that God is seeking to revive. John the Baptist uttered those words in relation to his ministry, not his identity. John's ministry was coming to an end as Jesus' ministry was just beginning. He had prepared the way of the Lord and now it was time for him to step out of the limelight. In no way is this a text that teaches that believers should deny their new identity in Christ. God's ardent desire is that you should become all that he made you to be, and therefore in relation to our new selves we should cry out, 'He should increase and I too should increase!' The more I am what he wants me to be, the more I will glorify him in my life.

Empty or full?

Go to any prayer meeting before a service or evangelistic event, and before too long you will hear someone pray something like this: 'Lord, when I speak tonight, don't let it be my words but let it be your words only.' Others make statements like: 'I just want to get myself out of the way so that God can work', or 'Don't let people see me, Lord. Let them only see you!'

Though they pray and speak with great sincerity and a real desire to honour God, their words express a false dualism that separates the human from the divine. In effect, they are saying that it is either God's work or man's, but not both. However, could it not be that man and God can work together in harmony? What if God delights in revealing himself in and through our very humanity? The key to understanding the union between the human and divine nature is the very person of Jesus Christ himself. 'In the beginning was the Word, and the Word was with God, and the Word was God. He was with God in the beginning' (John 1:1).

John begins his Gospel by affirming the divinity and pre-existence of the Word, who is Christ himself. John is proclaiming that Jesus Christ was fully divine but then goes on to express the mystery of the incarnation: 'The Word became flesh and made his dwelling among us.'

The eternal, omnipotent and divine Creator took upon himself our nature, and became a living, eating, breathing, feeling, thinking, Jewish man. The witness of the Scriptures is that Jesus Christ was fully man and fully God. By becoming man he did not become any less God, and being divine did not make him any less human. This is a great mystery to us and we cannot understand how it actually took place, but the New Testament writers are content to live with the mystery, confidently asserting that the two natures of Christ, the human and the divine, are brought together in perfect harmony in the one man, Jesus of Nazareth.

Now this is a supremely important point if we are to understand that we have a new nature, a real self, that is created by our union with God. We know that oil and water do not mix, that clay and iron cannot bond, but the incarnation of Jesus Christ proves beyond all shadow of doubt that you and I can be fully united to God himself. In this way we become brothers and sisters of Jesus Christ because we share the same nature. Just as Jesus Christ did not have to get rid of his humanity to reveal his divinity, so we also do not have to deny our earthly nature to reveal his presence in us.

I do not have to empty myself of my hopes and dreams, my talents and my gifts, nor do I have to assume that because I take pleasure in something I have to give it up as sinful. As we delight ourselves in the Lord he will give us the desires of our hearts, and we steadily become more full and complete than we were before. We are called to be full, not empty!

A journey into glory

When God's divine presence fills a man or woman, they are glorified (Romans 8:30) and begin the journey to completeness and full identity in Christ. This process of transformation takes place as we choose to let Christ fill every aspect of our entire beings. It is in Hindu and Buddhist thinking that we find the principle of the death of self. In Buddhism the self is snuffed out, the flame of individuality is extinguished; this is the principle of Nirvana. Hinduism teaches that though the self is not destroyed, it is absorbed into God. No longer a unique self, the soul is like a drop of rain returning to the ocean from which it came, and is lost in God. This is very far from Hebraic and biblical thinking, which teaches that the more filled with God we are, the more uniquely we become ourselves. As we die to the old, we live to the new. As we empty ourselves of all that is sinful and self-willed, God ignites that which is true and real, manifesting himself through the person's life.

At death we are not snuffed out, nor are we absorbed into God. St John puts it quite clearly in his first letter: 'But we know that when he appears, we shall be like him, for we shall see him as he is' (1 John 3:2). On Christ's return we shall be perfected into his likeness. We shall reveal the full glory of the union of God and man. We shall see him because we are distinct from him, and yet we shall be like him because we are in union with him. This is our glorious destiny. This is the manifestation of the true self. In the words of St Paul, we are to be 'filled to the measure of all the fullness of God' (Ephesians 3:19). What a vision of the glory, dignity and honour to be bestowed upon the children of God! Our destiny is almost too wonderful to imagine.

In his book *The Great Divorce* C. S. Lewis describes an allegorical dream in which he is on a journey towards heaven. The closer he gets to heaven, the more real are the things around him. The grass is painful to his feet, and the apples on the trees are too heavy to carry. Heaven is the place of absolute reality, and anything that does not share its reality is wispy and insubstantial. At one point he describes his first encounter with one of the Solid People:

> I had not yet looked one of the Solid People in the face. Now, when I did so, I discovered that one sees them with a kind of double vision. Here was an enthroned and shining god, whose ageless spirit weighed upon mine like a burden of solid gold: and yet, at the very same moment, here was an old weather-beaten man, one who might have been a shepherd . . . His eyes had the far-seeing look of one who has lived long in the open, solitary places; and somehow I divined the network of wrinkles which

must have surrounded them before re-birth had washed him in
immortality.[3]

Just as this 'old weather-beaten man' was washed in immortality, so are we who have been filled with the Spirit of God.
Lewis beautifully portrays the fulfilment of the true self in this
simple shepherd whose very human nature has been suffused
with the divine. He has now become a Solid Person in direct
contrast to the insubstantial and wispy Ghosts around him.
This is the real self that God is creating in each one of us. As
Irenaeus, a second-century theologian, said: 'The glory of God
is man fully alive, and the life of man is the vision of God.' We
become fully alive as all the human faculties are saturated with
his life and presence. Man in harmony with God is the com-
pletion of our true humanity.

Self-acceptance

Richard's struggle to express his true self was only partly the
result of a distorted understanding of what it meant to 'die to
self'. His theology was also wedded to his own inability to
accept himself. Richard did not like himself. Unaffirmed as a
child, he now struggled as an adult to see anything good
within himself, and therefore it was more comfortable for him
to think that he should put himself to death. His own particular brand of self-hatred underpinned his rejection of the true
self. If we reject ourselves, how then will we be able to allow
God to bless us and so reveal himself in us? We will be ignor-
ing and reviling those very characteristics that God loves,
through which he is wanting to radiate his presence and life.
Lack of self-acceptance will severely damage our growth to
fullness in Christ.

Ashley and Sandy also struggle with self-acceptance but in different ways. Ashley needs to be the life and soul of the party. He desperately needs to be successful. These are the masks that he has created over the years to hide the inner emptiness and anxiety. He has developed a 'false persona' that is denying the true self. To come into maturity and wholeness, he will have to disengage himself from his masks and look up to God to tell him who he is. In the presence of God's loving attention and healing words, the true Ashley will emerge.

Sandy will have to do the same, but her starting point is rather different. Ashley is out of touch with his feelings and is living 'from the neck up', but Sandy is overwhelmed by her emotions. Her feelings dominate her life. Anxiety, fear and self-hatred oppress her daily. She has withdrawn within herself and is terrified to emerge. She too must come up and out of the dark hole that she is living in. She must choose to change and grow and to embrace the true woman that God has made her to be. This will be as painful for her as it is for Ashley, but in the light of God's presence and truth they will be able to grow to maturity and wholeness.

Hiding behind masks

If we do not know what it means to accept ourselves, we will try to create an identity that will enable us to survive. Instead of living out of a solid sense of identity and being, we try to become what we think others will approve of. Never feeling at home within ourselves, we will strive to become a person who is liked and valuable. Figure 1 shows how the real self, the grey figure, stays small and hidden while the false self grows larger and more rigid.[4]

Behind the mask it is empty and lonely, but we keep it in

place to give ourselves some sense of identity. Our masks develop over time, and little by little the false self becomes our identity. Without us realising what is taking place, we become someone far removed from God's original design. Our masks may offer some protection and identity, but they separate us from God and from one another.

Learning to accept oneself

What does it mean to accept myself? Fundamentally it involves coming to a place of engaged acceptance of every aspect of ourselves – our intellects, emotions, imaginations, personality traits and also our bodies.

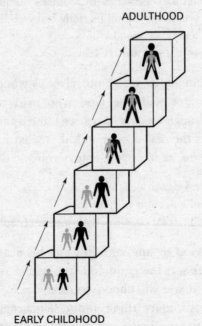

ADULTHOOD

EARLY CHILDHOOD

Figure 1 – The hidden self

Self-acceptance is gained through facing those very aspects of ourselves that we have denied, ignored or rejected, and in the presence of God, listening for his loving words of blessing and affirmation, we learn to embrace ourselves as he has done. We learn to say of ourselves, 'By the grace of God I am what I am' (1 Corinthians 15:10). Seeing ourselves in the light of God's love and truth, our hearts are healed and we allow his presence to flood and saturate those very things that we have hated. In this way we become the person that God made us to be. We are able to confess from the bottom of our hearts the words of Psalm 139:

> For you created my inmost being;
>> you knit me together in my mother's womb.
> I praise you because I am fearfully and wonderfully made;
>> your works are wonderful,
>> I know that full well. (v.13)

It is true humility to accept ourselves as wonderful, for in so doing we agree with the God who made us. We are his creatures; though we may have been tainted and twisted by sin, he perceives the real person and likes what he sees. God not only loves you, he likes you, enjoys you and delights in you.

> He will take great delight in you,
>> he will quiet you with his love,
>> he will rejoice over you with singing. (Zephaniah 3:17)

You cause God to sing with joy, and his heart to swell with pleasure! He sees the good and true within you and is ready to bless it – if you will choose to receive it.

The extraordinary thing about self-acceptance is that it enables us to stop being self-centred and selfish. Once I am able to accept myself in the light of God's full acceptance of me, then I no longer need to analyse myself, compare myself, protect myself or prove myself. I become free to serve, free to love, free to bless.

> The act of self-acceptance is the root of all things. I must agree to be the person who I am. Agree to have the qualifications which I have. Agree to live within the limitations set for me . . . The clarity and the courageousness of this acceptance is the foundation of all existence.[5]

In my own life I have struggled to accept myself. This has manifested itself in a restless striving to be good enough for others to accept. Feeling inadequate in intellect, personality and stature, I would continually compare myself to other men and would quickly condemn myself. Analysing my character and performance was an established habit pattern. I wore different hats to please different people and found it extremely hard simply to be myself. God might love me, but I did not like myself. I understood the reality of the following:

> We are not what we think we are.
> We are not what others think we are.
> We are what we think others think we are.

I did not know who I was, and I certainly did not know who God thought I was. As I rejected myself so I suppressed the person God made me to be. I felt wispy and insubstantial, much like the Ghosts in C. S. Lewis's *The Great Divorce*. As I have dared to face who I am and to renounce the masks that I have developed, so I have learnt to receive God's blessing on those things that I once rejected in myself. It has been a painful but wonderful journey.

I am now in a place which, though far from perfect, is a place of freedom and rest. I am able to be me. No longer analysing myself, no longer distracted by what others think of me, I am able to lift my eyes to the Lord and find my identity in him. I am much more self-aware than I used to be, in that I have had to face my own heart and its twisted and compulsive desires, but I am now less self-absorbed. Knowing that I am loved, accepted and good in his eyes has enabled me to look away from myself to him and to the needs of those around me.

In accepting myself as the man that God has made, I have come to enjoy my strengths and to accept my limitations; both of them are God-given. I have by no means come to a point where I do not struggle to stay at ease and at peace, but I have tasted it, I have begun to walk in it. I am able simply to 'be', and the old restlessness and need to prove myself is being replaced by a new peace and contentment. I have looked into the abyss of my own heart and found that God himself is present in the darkness as well as the light. Knowing that he has accepted me, I have dared to accept myself, and in that process allowed his radiating and transforming love to change me. I am learning to be real.

Loved into reality

'There once was a Velveteen Rabbit, and in the beginning he was really splendid.' So begins Margery Williams' enchanting and insightful story, *The Velveteen Rabbit*. One Christmas morning he was given to the Boy, and to begin with he was dearly loved. In the nursery there were many other toys who snubbed him and looked down on him. The mechanical toys were very superior and pretended that they were real. But the Velveteen Rabbit was shy and had no idea that real rabbits existed; he thought all rabbits were stuffed with sawdust. The poor little rabbit felt very ordinary and insignificant. The only toy who liked him was the Skin Horse, who had lived in the nursery for many years and was very wise.

'What is REAL?' asked the Rabbit one day, when they were lying side by side near the nursery fender. 'Does it mean having things that buzz inside you and a stick-out handle?'

'Real isn't how you are made,' said the Skin Horse. 'It's a thing that happens to you. When a child loves you for a long, long time, not just to play with, but REALLY loves you, then you become real.'

'Does it hurt?' asked the Rabbit.

'Sometimes,' said the Skin Horse, for he was always truthful. 'When you are real you don't mind being hurt.'

'Does it happen all at once, like being wound up,' he asked, 'or bit by bit?'

'It doesn't happen all at once,' said the Skin Horse. 'You become. It takes a long time.'[6]

Like the Velveteen Rabbit and the Skin Horse, we become real as we are loved. REALLY loved. We are all able to become Real and Solid People as we live in the light and warmth of God's love. If we are courageous enough to enter God's real presence, and there renounce the masks and dare to be naked, vulnerable and transparent, we will come to see ourselves as he sees us. In his presence there is grace to renounce the false self and to embrace the true self.

In Colossians, Paul expresses this place of refuge and acceptance when he says: 'For you died [the old self in separation] and your life is now hidden with Christ in God. When Christ, who is your life, appears, then you also will appear with him in glory' (Colossians 3:3–4).

Like an unborn child safe in the acceptance and refuge of the womb, so we are embraced and sustained with Christ in God. We are not to hide ourselves *from* God but to hide ourselves *in* God. Imbued with his life and glory, we grow to become restored images of the living God and the true self becomes more real and solid than we ever thought possible.

The purpose of the real self

We are being recreated to fulfil God's calling on our lives. I am being transformed, not to serve myself but to love God with all my heart, all my mind, all my soul and all my strength. This is what you and I have been made for – to honour God and to give our lives in loving abandonment to his will and his purposes. As I allow God to love me and as I give myself to loving him back, so my life glorifies him. Think of a spotlight. It is full of light and its beam lights up that upon which it shines. So it is with us: as we are filled with light and love so we glorify the Lord. The more full we are of his presence, the more we will point away from ourselves to him. No one gazes at a spotlight; they watch to see what it is shining upon. You and I were made, not to draw attention to ourselves, but to glorify God.

As we enjoy God's love towards us, and as we love him back with everything within us, so we will grow in his love and in his likeness. This is our aim: to love God and to reveal his presence in us through every little detail in our lives. We are made real, not to bless ourselves but to give glory to the One who has given us his life and his love.

Father God, I thank you that you know me, that you love me and that you accept me as I am. Thank you that you dwell within me. I choose to begin to accept myself as the man/woman whom you have made. Please give me courage to put down the masks and to be open and vulnerable before you.

I choose to become all that you have made me to be in order that my life might glorify you, the one and only true God. Amen.

EXERCISES

1. Write out those aspects of yourself that you like and those that you dislike.
    Likes:
    Dislikes:

2. What masks do you put on?

3. Irenaeus said that 'the glory of God is man fully alive'. In what ways could you be fully alive?

4. Meditate on Zephaniah 3:17. Now consciously choose to see yourself as precious and wonderful in God's eyes and invite the Holy Spirit to fill and saturate every part of your being.

2
The Wonderful Riches of His Grace

In 1941, during the Second World War, a young English pilot was shot down over the Norfolk coast. As his Lancaster bomber crashed into the sea, the lifeboat was launched from the nearby village of Wells. Sadly, they never found the young pilot and the crewmen abandoned the search, presuming him to be drowned. His fiancée was utterly distraught when she heard the news. Having loved and lost her young pilot, she resolved never to marry; she died in November 1995, still heartbroken and still unmarried, at the age of eighty-seven. Margaret did not die penniless, and in a gesture to remember her fiancé she left her inheritance to the crew of the 1995 Wells lifeboat. To their utter surprise they discovered that they had £400,000 to share! None of them took part in the original rescue mission, yet they came to share in an inheritance that they had not earned.

Can you imagine the surprise and delight those crewmen must have felt at learning the news of their inheritance? They were stunned and amazed at their good fortune.

Riches in Christ

For us who confess the name of Christ the surprise and amazement at our inheritance is no less great. In fact it should be far greater! When we made our first steps to respond to Christ and accept him as our Lord and Saviour, none of us knew the extent of the glorious riches we would receive from his grace. We have received eternal riches and spiritual blessings that far outweigh anything that man can devise or even imagine.

> Praise be to the God and Father of our Lord Jesus Christ who has blessed us in the heavenly realms with every spiritual blessing in Christ. (Ephesians 1:3)

Read that verse again. God is revealing to us through St Paul that he has poured out upon us 'every spiritual blessing in Christ'. Now, the word 'every' means what it says! The Father has supplied us with everything we could possibly want or need to live full and effective lives for him. It is a glorious adventure to discover all that is ours in Christ. No single person has ever explored and experienced all the spiritual blessings that Christ has won for us by his life, death and resurrection. There is always more to take hold of!

It is God who has pioneered the work of re-creation within us, and it is only as we understand what God has done for us in Christ that we will have a solid foundation on which to build our lives. True personhood and identity is only found by becoming all that God has made us to be: if our understanding of his work in us is deficient, so too will be our growth to maturity. Just as God told Abraham to journey through the land that he had already promised to give him, so we too need to explore the wonderful riches of his grace if we are to take hold of them in our lives.

Sadly, many of us find the riches of the world more attractive and easier to take hold of than the riches of Christ. The extent to which we take hold of the 'spiritual blessings' will depend on how much we value them and how much we seek them. All these blessings are already ours. This is not a distant hope for the future – it is a present reality. Read the verse above again: 'who *has* blessed us in the heavenly realms'. The verb 'has blessed' is past tense. We already have them, they are ours now, and if we choose to seek them with all our heart, soul, mind and strength, then they will become living truth to us. God's truth is not meant to be pie in the sky when you die, but meat on your plate while you wait!

Lasting riches

The world's riches appeal to our old sinful nature, but so do the spiritual blessings appeal to our spiritual nature. Our spiritual nature hungers after spiritual realities. It is normal for the Western mind to consider spiritual realities less real and less solid than the material realities of this world. The phrase 'spiritual blessings' seems somehow less of an objective reality than money in the bank, a luxurious holiday or the house of your dreams, but our concept of spiritual things is so diminished and limited. Spiritual realities are more solid and more real than the riches of this world! This world and its desires are passing away (1 John 2:17) but the spiritual realm will last for ever.

Let me ask you a question. Is God more real than you, or are you more real than God? God is spirit and you and I are flesh and blood. If we assume that the physical, material realm is more real than the spirit realm, then you and I are more real than God. But God is spirit, he is fourth-dimensional reality (and, I imagine, fifth- and sixth- and seventh-dimensional too!) and he created us. He existed before us, brought us into being and will go on existing long after this world has been destroyed. Only that which is spirit will last for eternity. Only those men and women born of the Spirit will last for eternity. Therefore, by definition, 'spiritual realities' are more solid, more lasting and more concrete than three-dimensional material realities. Don't be fooled by the mindset of this materialistic age. Just because you can't see or touch spiritual realities with your natural senses does not mean they are less substantial than those things you can see and touch. Ask God to open afresh your spiritual eyes and your spiritual senses to see the riches and blessings of his kingdom. 'So we fix our eyes not on what is seen, but on what is unseen. For what is seen is temporary, but what is unseen is eternal' (2 Corinthians 4:18).

As we take hold of these unseen riches that the Father lavishes on us, then we become more substantial men and women. Eternal realities pervade our beings, and we too become more and more like Christ as we participate in his divine nature (2 Peter 1:4).

Let's look now at these incomparable (Ephesians 2:7), unsearchable (Ephesians 3:8) and glorious (Colossians 1:27) riches that we have inherited through Jesus Christ. We will look at them under three headings – that we are chosen, we are forgiven and we are indwelt.

We are chosen

God chose Abraham, Moses, David and the people of the nation of Israel because he loved them. The same is true today. God chooses us because he loves us. We own the name of

Christ because God chose us first to know him and to love him. In John 15:16 Jesus proclaimed, 'You did not choose me, but I chose you.' Each one of us was lost in sin, our eyes were blind to his truth and our spirits were dead within us until the Father, having chosen us before the creation of the world (Ephesians 1:4), searched us out (John 4:23), found us and drew us to himself, and then enabled us to receive his gift of life with faith (Ephesians 2:8).

To understand that we are chosen is good theology. It recognises that God always takes the initiative in the work of salvation and that none of us can boast that we found God! We love him only because he first loved us (1 John 4:10). Knowing that we are chosen exalts God's sovereignty and free will and also diminishes man's egotistical view of himself. We like to think we can determine our destiny, that we are the captain of our own fate, and it is a very great blow to our pride when we realise that we contributed nothing to our eternal destiny, other than our sin (Ephesians 2:3–4).

Who chose who?

Now you could point out to me that we all have free will to respond to or reject the good news of Christ, and you would be right! The Bible asserts that God is sovereign and that he chose us first, but it also teaches that we must respond to the message with faith (Mark 1:15). Scripture does not try to reconcile these two concepts and is happy to live with the mystery that both principles are true at the same time! The Western mind, rooted in Greek thought patterns, wants to establish a framework of truth that is logical and explicable and within which mystery is an unwelcome stranger. On the other hand, Hebrew thinking was rooted in the understanding that truth could only be found through relationship with God. The

Israelite mind was content to accept mystery, because mystery lay at the heart of the nature and character of a God who was above and beyond the grasp of man's limited thinking.

Both principles are true at the same time. It is humbling for us to have to live with a mystery that is perfectly clear to the mind of God but which defies our attempts to define it and box it to fit our neat doctrinal constructions. You were chosen by God long before you made a decision to follow him.

To know in our hearts and minds that we are chosen brings truth to the deep places of our hearts and satisfies a profound emotional need within us. Every person needs to know they are wanted, chosen and loved. To be denied such knowledge causes deep anxiety and pain. To find a place of safety in an unsafe world I must know that there is someone who wants me and chooses me for their own. When we have revelation to our hearts that this person is none other than the almighty, loving and eternal God, then we have a genuine foundation for a consistent and joyful walk with him.

Roger and Kim got married because Kim was pregnant. It was a shotgun marriage, conducted against the back-drop of much pressure and guilt. For Kim, the fact that Roger might not have chosen her but for the pregnancy has caused her much stress and anxiety. She is unsure that she was his chosen one, unsure that she was chosen before all others, and she fears that maybe he did the decent thing out of duty and not out of love. If our relationship with God is not rooted in a secure heartfelt conviction that he chose us, then we too will be uncertain of his utter commitment to fulfil the work that he has begun in us.

God chose you because he loves you. From before the foundation of the world, he planned to bring you to himself. He chose you not because he had to, or even needed to, but because he wanted to, because he loves you with a great passion. 'In love he predestined us to be adopted as his sons [and daughters] through Jesus Christ, in accordance with his pleasure and will' (Ephesians 1:5).

God took great pleasure in choosing you, and he made it happen by willing it in the spirit realm. In the light of all this, we can REST! We can rest from striving to be accepted or from striving to be chosen. The fear that we might be rejected, like a child waiting to be picked for a sports team, need not grip us and bind us. If we do not know in our hearts that we are chosen out of love, then we will for ever seek to prove that we are worth choosing. We will lose sight of grace and end up working hard to earn his love. In Part 2, we will look in more depth at our ability to embrace this truth, and the obstacles we may encounter. If you are finding it hard to enjoy the riches of this truth – that you are wanted, sought after and chosen by God – there is hope. You can know it and it will bring you rest and peace!

We are forgiven

The cross is the most critical moment for mankind in all of history. It is the place where the grace of God was fully revealed and the place from which grace was fully released. Without the grace of God making forgiveness freely available to you and me, we would for ever be separated from the source of all life. Eternal death would have been our only future. 'For Christ died for sins once for all, the righteous for the unrighteous, to bring you to God' (1 Peter 3:18). Our inheritance, therefore, is not death but life! Forgiveness has opened for us the doorway into life, in all its abundance. No wonder Paul includes forgiveness in his list of spiritual blessings in Ephesians 1:7. 'In him we have redemption through his blood, the forgiveness of sins, in accordance with the riches of God's grace that he lavished on us with all wisdom and understanding.'

Sadly, many believers do not truly enjoy the riches of knowing that they are utterly forgiven. I once heard John White, the author and speaker, say that in his opinion '95 per cent of all Christians are rendered ineffective for service, because they have not grasped the principle that the death of Jesus is enough'.

At the beginning of that wonderful film *The Mission*, a young Spaniard kills his brother in a fight over a woman. His desperate act leaves him in great torment, and in order to expunge his guilt he loads a net with rocks and carries it around as a penance. Until we have personal revelation from the Spirit of God that we are completely, utterly, totally and unceasingly forgiven, we too will try and work off our guilt. We will carry around our own 'rocks', shaped to fit our own particular circumstances and personalities. One person may try to pray more in order to feel more acceptable to God, while another may tirelessly serve their local church out of a need to prove their devotion to God and feel more 'forgivable'. Each one of us has ways in which we try to earn our own forgiveness, even though we may know all the relevant Scripture verses in our heads. We need to ask the Holy Spirit to show us what 'rocks' we are carrying around; if you are not aware of them at present, it is almost certain that they will be motivating you at an unseen level. The truth is that all our attempts to be worthy of forgiveness are quite useless and only prevent us depending on the once-for-all sacrifice of Jesus: 'All of us have become like one who is unclean, and all our righteous acts are like filthy rags' (Isaiah 64:6)

Until we end our futile attempts to improve our standing before a holy God, we will never stop long enough to receive the revelation that we so desperately need. His forgiveness is a free gift that each of us must simply and humbly receive with thanks.

Revelation brings reality

What is revelation? How can I receive revelation of my forgiveness? Revelation is the opening of the spiritual eyes of the inner being to the reality of the truth of God's Word (Ephesians 1:18). Revelation only comes about by a work of the Spirit that enables the heart to accept, receive and enjoy the reality of God's Word. Knowledge is not necessarily revelation, for knowledge can remain as information only. The word 'revelation' in Greek is *apokalupto*, meaning 'to uncover' or 'unveil'.[1] Revelation occurs when the Holy Spirit imparts his truth to the head and the heart. We come into a place of knowing that we have not enjoyed before. We find a place of deep conviction.

Many Christians can quote chapter and verse on forgiveness, but when it comes to entering the presence of God they find themselves withdrawing out of unworthiness and guilt. I recently spent time with a young man, Robert, who was experiencing unpleasant reactions to the presence of the Holy Spirit. As we talked he began to confess some vile and sinful things that he had done as a boy and as a young man. At one level he had come to terms with his guilt, but only by silencing his conscience. He knew in his head that his sins were forgiven, but because in his heart he had not truly faced these things as sin and therefore offensive to God, his body manifested the shame and guilt his inner being felt when the Spirit of God began to touch him. He knew the verses that I read to him, but they were still only information and had not yet become revelation.

I asked Robert to close his eyes and see the cross in his imagination. I knew that by trying to picture the cross, he would see it in a way that revealed his heart. Sure enough, he saw the cross, with Jesus on it, but it was far away on top of a hill. It was not that God hadn't forgiven Robert, but rather that Robert had yet to embrace the fullness of his forgiveness in Christ. I then asked the Holy Spirit to bring revelation to Robert and, praying silently, I waited for revelation to come. After a while, he opened his eyes and said, 'The cross came closer and closer, and then for a split second Jesus' feet were by my cheek as I knelt before him.' Over the next few days, as Robert held on to Scripture verses about forgiveness and imagined the cross beside him, he was able to take hold of Jesus' feet and 'see' the blood of Christ cleanse him. In this way he was able to have revelation, to both his head and his heart. The fact that God had utterly forgiven him and that Jesus' blood had been shed for him became a living reality – information had turned into revelation!

Have you received revelation to your own mind and heart that Jesus Christ's blood was shed for you? That his death is enough for you? When you sin, do you still find yourself shrinking back from prayer or praise? If you do not run straight into the presence of the Lord when you sin (be it the first time for a while or the hundredth time that day), then you need to seek God for a greater revelation of the forgiveness that he won for you on the cross (Hebrews 4:15–16).

The riches of forgiveness enable us to enter the very presence of our holy and majestic God. When we are struggling with sin, weakness and temptation, we can be bold and confident, for he will not turn us away and we will receive mercy and strengthening power to overcome and defeat the things we battle against. Later in this book we will go into more depth on how we can receive revelation of truth. If this is an area you struggle with, or that is new to you, it may well be worth reading Chapter 12 right now.

We are indwelt

Sitting among a small group of teenagers being prepared for their confirmation, I asked them the question, 'What makes someone a Christian?' After a short silence they began to offer their thoughts: 'being loved by God', 'being forgiven', 'being accepted by God', 'being chosen by God'. I readily acknowledged that these were all excellent ideas and rooted in the Bible, but suggested that none of them actually made a person a Christian. Paul, in Romans 8:9–11, says:

> You, however, are controlled not by the sinful nature but by the Spirit, if the Spirit of God lives in you. And if anyone does not have the Spirit of Christ, he does not belong to Christ. But if Christ is in you, your body is dead because of sin, yet your spirit is alive because of righteousness. And if the Spirit of him who raised Jesus from the dead is living in you, he who raised Christ from the dead will also give life to your mortal bodies through his Spirit, who lives in you.

Five times in that passage Paul speaks of God's presence indwelling us. He uses different phrases to describe this spiritual reality. We are indwelt by the Spirit of God (v.9), the Spirit of Christ (v.9), Christ (v.10), the Spirit of him who raised Jesus from the dead (v. 11), his Spirit (v. 11). Paul states that the only people who belong to Christ are those in whom God has come to dwell.

Being chosen and being forgiven by God are riches indeed, but they pave the way for the man or woman to receive the greatest riches of all – the riches of being united with, and indwelt by, the eternal, almighty and ever-loving God. This is the only source of eternal life for mortal man and without it we are devoid of life. Like the branches that Jesus spoke of in John 15, we will wither and die when we are separated from the one true Vine.

Jesus' statement to Nicodemus, that unless he is born again he will not enter the kingdom of God, reveals that a radical change in his human nature needs to take place. In John 14:23 Jesus puts it plainly: 'If anyone loves me, he will obey my teaching. My Father will love him, and we will come to him and make our home with him.'

At my conversion God himself came to live within me. He took up permanent residence within my body, soul and spirit. I have therefore become a 'temple of the Holy Spirit' (1 Corinthians 6:19). I have died to the old self and am now a new person. My new nature is given to me by my total identification with him who is divine.

> I have been crucified with Christ [the old me, living in separation from God, is dead] and I [the old me] no longer live, but Christ lives in me [Christ in me – the new person brought to life!]. The life I live in the body [I now live a new kind of life within my body] I live by faith [trusting him always] in the Son of God who loved me and gave himself for me [the cross opened the way for me to take hold of this new life].

This is the greatest truth in all the universe! Left to ourselves we wither and die, but God chose us, forgave us and then unites himself with us so that his life becomes our life and we live new lives as new people. We are truly new creations in

Christ (2 Corinthians 5:17). C. S. Lewis describes this transformation as being as great as if 'a statue changed from being carved stone to being a real man'.[2]

The first verse I ever memorised was Galatians 2:20. It was not until ten years later that I had revelation as to its true meaning! Two weeks after beginning my first curacy at an Anglican church in Essex, I went to a conference held in the church by Clay McClean. These were three of the most momentous days of my life, for during them I received such wonderful revelations from the Holy Spirit that my life was never to be the same. The first bombshell to hit me was understanding that Christ dwelt in *me*! Clay told a story about his friend, the author Leanne Payne.

One Christmas Eve, Leanne was in her kitchen, chopping up vegetables for the next day's meal. The phone rang and as she answered it a desperate voice asked, 'Is that Leanne Payne?'

'Yes,' she replied.

'I hear you pray for people and they get healed. Can I come round now?' Leanne quickly prayed. Sensing the Holy Spirit's affirmation, she said, 'OK, come round.' To her surprise, the man then exclaimed, 'Thank you, but you see I'm a rabbi and I need to ask you not to mention the name Jesus!' So Leanne promised not to talk about Jesus, only to pray in his name. Satisfied, the rabbi hung up and made his way to Leanne's apartment (and she went back to chopping her vegetables).

When the doorbell rang, she went to open the door, at the same time inviting Jesus to be present at the meeting. The rabbi walked in, but as he did so he began to shout, 'JESUS! JESUS! JESUS!' This man, steeped in rabbinical teaching, who never mentioned the name Jesus, was now shouting it aloud in Leanne's doorway! As he finished shouting, he fell down under the power of the Holy Spirit and lay on her hall floor for two hours. Meanwhile Leanne went back to chopping her vegetables!

Leanne heard him uttering wonderful truths that the Spirit of God was releasing in him as all the rich Jewish learning came alive under the impact of the Spirit of God. When he finally emerged from this spiritual state, Leanne asked him about it. 'What happened?' she said.

'As I walked through your door,' he replied, 'I saw Jesus standing behind you. He walked right past you and towards me, and it was then that I began to shout his name. He kept on walking towards me, closer and closer, until he walked right INTO me!' Of all the statements he made under the influence of this profound encounter, the one that made the greatest impression on Leanne was this: 'I now understand that grace is not a principle but a person!'

Incarnational reality

This story had a real impact on me. What had been a concept I 'believed' now became a living truth. If Christ was living *in* me, then Christ could live his life out *through* me. If I was indwelt and joined to him, then living a full and victorious Christian life became a genuine possibility! I am a person who thinks primarily in pictures, and this story had enabled my heart and mind to receive revelation of the biblical passages my intellect knew so well. In her books, Leanne Payne uses a very helpful phrase to describe the presence of Christ within a believer: she calls it 'incarnational reality'. She describes how the Christian is indwelt and fundamentally changed by the real presence of the Spirit of God incarnating himself in the believer's spirit, soul and body. Christ dwells in my spirit and your spirit, in my soul and your soul, in my body and your body. You and I are home to the living God!

Counterfeit truth

Now, at this point I need to state that this is not New Age/Eastern religion teaching. As New Age teaching spreads, it urges people to realise their own 'godness'. Believing God to be everywhere and to be in everything, they assert that we too are gods and that therefore the secret to life is to realise and release your own 'godness'. This is counterfeit truth; while apparently similar to the New Testament's teaching on our new nature in Christ, it is fundamentally different. I am not God, or even a part of God. I was a sinner separated from God by my sin. Through the cross I am forgiven and by his grace I am now indwelt. He who is holy, eternal, all-knowing, all-wise and all-powerful condescends to come and live within me, a mere human who is temporal, sinful, limited, weak and foolish. New Age teaching and biblical truth may sound similar but they are light years apart in their basic understanding of man's condition. Man is a sinner in need of a saviour, not a god in need of releasing his divine potential!

It is because we are in Christ and receive our identity from him that we are able to grow into full maturity and become solid and complete. To know that he has chosen us, forgiven us and indwelt us is the foundation upon which we can build our lives and through which the real self can begin to emerge.

Father God, I thank you from the bottom of my heart for the wonderful riches you have poured upon my life. I choose to rest in the knowledge that you have chosen me, to enjoy the freedom of forgiveness and to walk in the power of your indwelling presence. Please give me ever-deepening revelation of these wonderful realities, and show me where I fail to live in their liberating truth. Amen.

EXERCISES

1. Read Ephesians 1:4, 'For he chose us in him before the creation of the world.' What difference does it make to you to know that he chose you to be his child?

2. In what ways do you try to earn God's forgiveness? Is there any unresolved guilt within you, needing a revelation of his forgiveness? Meditate on 1 John 1:9. Choose to believe God's Word above your feelings.

3. Place your hand on your heart and welcome the Holy Spirit into every part of your spirit, soul and body. Spend time resting in his presence.

4. Spend a few moments thanking God for the riches of his grace that he has lavished upon you.

3

Will the Real Me Please Stand Up

Sitting beside the hospital bed, Martha and I watched and prayed as Aristide struggled for his life. I could sense Martha's longing that the day of the heart operation would come soon, for she knew that without it her husband was sure to die. The very next day a donor was found, and within three days Aristide was up and about. It was an amazing transformation! No longer weak and pathetic, he was walking round the ward, cracking jokes and asking for steak and chips. Martha's relief was palpable and the worry lines etched into her face were beginning to fade away.

The Old Testament prophets longed for a day when hearts would be changed. They ached for God to have a people who would no longer be rebellious, faithless and stubborn, but obedient, loving and trustworthy. They looked forward to a time when the Spirit of God would not simply rest upon men and women but would actually indwell their hearts and transform them:

> I will give you a new heart and put a new spirit within you. I will remove from you your heart of stone and give you a heart of flesh. And I will put my Spirit within you and move you to follow my decrees and be careful to keep my laws. (Ezekiel 36:26)

The fulfilment of this prophetic longing was realised on the day of Pentecost, when the church was filled with the life and power of the Holy Spirit. Two thousand years later, we still proclaim 'the glorious riches of this mystery, which is *Christ in you*, the hope of glory' (Colossians 1:27, italics mine).

The essence of the good news is that God and man are now reconciled and able to dwell in peace and spiritual union. Having come to dwell within us, his purpose is to release his life into every level of our being: spirit, soul and body.

Spirit, soul and body

Each person has a spirit, soul and body. These three aspects of our existence are distinct and yet united within us. We cannot separate ourselves to see where one begins and another ends, for they are deeply interwoven within the very fabric of our humanity. Spirit, soul and body comprise the trinity of man.

The spirit (*pneuma*) is the deepest level of existence within man. Made in the image of God, man is a spirit being. Apart from Christ the human spirit is lifeless and ineffectual, but in union with Christ the human spirit is revived and man experiences rebirth.

The soul (*psyche*) describes the inner nature of man and includes our mind, our emotions, our personality traits and our wills.

The body (*soma*) relates to our physical nature, and includes all aspects of our corporeal existence – arms, legs, spine, brain . . .

The spiritual man

In the spiritual man (1 Corinthians 2:15), God's Spirit has entered at the deepest level of his being and brought the human spirit alive. The man's spirit is now in union with God, and consequently we come to participate in the divine nature (2 Peter 1:4). Eternity is breathed into us. God's creative power restores to us the capacity to become all that he created us to be, and his presence begins to pervade every part of the soul and the body. We are now able to live as his 'workmanship in Christ Jesus' (Ephesians 2:10).

This is the miracle of transformation that takes place when God's life comes to live within us. This is what happened to Leanne Payne's rabbi. We who were dead are now alive, and at the very centre of our nature is the eternal and substantial presence of God himself. We become new people with a new nature and a new identity.

The new nature

Therefore, if anyone is in Christ, he is a new creation; the old has gone, the new has come! (2 Corinthians 5:17)

Because we are now 'in Christ', Paul reveals that we are 'new creations'. He does not say that we are becoming new creations, he states that we *have become* new creations. Past tense! In other words, we were radically transformed at the moment Jesus Christ came to live within us by his Spirit. Just as a woman cannot be a little bit pregnant, so we cannot be a little bit Christian. We either are indwelt by the Holy Spirit, or we are not! I am a new creation because a new person has come to live within me. The 'old self', that self which lived separate from God's life-giving presence, is dead. That old life is finished, it is ended, it is over and done with. A new person has been created, one who now shares in the very life of God himself. This new person is the true self that lives in union with God and has the power and capacity to live like Christ day by day.

> For we know that our old self was crucified with him so that the body of sin might be done away with. (Romans 6:6)

> I no longer live, but Christ lives in me. (Galatians 2:20)

> But God, who is rich in mercy, made us alive with Christ. (Ephesians 2:4)

This, then, is the foundational truth on which the whole of our new life in Christ is to be lived. We are new creations because God has come to live at the very core of every person who humbly receives him by faith. The implications of this reality are quite amazing, because God imparts to us, through the indwelling Spirit, all the riches and qualities that are to be found in the person of Jesus Christ. 'For in Christ all the fullness of the Deity lives in bodily form, and you have been given fullness in Christ' (Colossians 2:9).

BODY

SOUL

HUMAN SPIRIT & HOLY SPIRIT

Figure 2 – The spiritual man

Every aspect of the nature of the Son of God is given to every believer. The language of this blessing is always past tense. We *have been* given fullness in Christ. Because of the decisive work of the cross, which paid for our sin once for all, and because of the equally decisive act of incarnation within our spirits, we are able to build our new lives upon a solid foundation. The old *has* gone, the new *has* come and we are for ever changed.

Father God, thank you that Jesus Christ has come to live within me by the presence of the Holy Spirit. Thank you that I am now a new creation. Please open my eyes and my heart to see and understand all that you have given me through his indwelling presence. I choose to accept this as truth and to no longer see myself from a worldly perspective. Amen.

We are holy

If you were to be asked whether you were a holy person, how would you respond? Most people would shuffle awkwardly, consider the state of their lives and answer immediately, 'Of course I am not holy!'

When Paul wrote to the Ephesians, he began his letter by addressing them as 'the saints who live in Ephesus' (Ephesians 1:1). In the New Testament, believers are frequently called saints (Romans 8:27; 1 Corinthians 6:2; Ephesians 6:18; Philemon 7; Revelation 19:8). The word means 'holy one' in the original Greek. Paul is addressing them as 'the holy ones in Ephesus'!

Does this mean that their lives were perfect without fault or sin? Not at all. Paul regularly rebukes the believers for their ungodly behaviour. What he is doing is addressing the Christians according to their new nature. He knows that they are more than just forgiven. God has gone one step beyond forgiveness, and has actually made the people holy at the very core of their existence. Their new nature is pure, without blemish, and cannot sin. In the same way, you and I have been made holy by the presence of Christ within us.

I remember being taught as a new believer that God, who is the source of all holiness, could not look at me because I was still a sinner. To solve the problem, so I was told, he looked at me through Jesus instead. The logical outcome of such teaching is that I felt like a corpse covered by a beautiful garment – Jesus, covering my sinfulness. Forgiveness was in fact a kind of 'legal fiction' by which God called me clean, knowing full well that I was still as sinful as before. God therefore played a game of pretend, in which he declared me righteous while I was still alive, but was waiting to get me to heaven when he could make me perfect and complete. This teaching on forgiveness is widespread in the church, and leaves believers with little hope of being truly changed in this life. It is a doctrine that comes from an over-emphasis on the cross and an under-emphasis on the resurrection and impartation of the Spirit. It is one thing to be forgiven and declared righteous by God, but it is a greater truth that God has actually made you righteous and holy in your new nature.

> But you are a chosen people, a royal priesthood, *a holy nation*, a people belonging to God. (1 Peter 2:9, italics mine)

> For he chose us in him before the creation of the world to be *holy and blameless* in his sight. (Ephesians 1:4, italics mine)

Having been made holy by his holy presence within us, we are called to live out that same purity in our daily lives. We do not strive to become holy by our behaviour; that is the way of law. It is only because we have been made holy that we can live lives that display his presence within us. To be holy has two central meanings. First, it means utter purity as found in the person of God. Second, it means to be separated unto God. The first aspect we receive through being new creations, but the second aspect, that of living lives separated from the world's ways, is the ongoing challenge of the Christ-centred life. 'You ought to live holy and godly lives' (2 Peter 3:11).

Pictorially it looks like Figure 3. Your new nature is holy because God himself is holy and he dwells within you. As a transformed person you can now live a life of holiness that is pleasing to the Father. What an extraordinary work of grace!

You are spiritual

Johnny had been struggling to understand how it is that a human being, made of physical matter, could know and experience an invisible and spiritual God. He was intellectually convinced of the truth of the Christian faith, and this was his one remaining hurdle to committing his life to Christ.

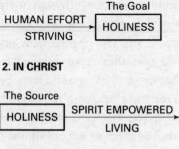

Figure 3 – Your new nature

Clasping and unclasping his hands, he wrestled with the problem. 'You cannot work this out for yourself, Johnny. Only God can do it for you. His Spirit will enable you to do what you cannot do on your own.'

Moments later he invited Jesus into his heart as his Lord and Saviour, still struggling with uncertainty but stepping out in faith. At the very moment of praying, large tears began to flow down his cheeks, a huge grin spread across his face and without him saying a word, it was clear that he now knew what his rational mind had been unable to grasp before. His spirit had come to life through the presence of the Lord, and he had met with God, spirit to Spirit.

Jesus said, 'Flesh gives birth to flesh, but spirit gives birth to spirit.' Now that we are in Christ, we have become spiritual beings. I am a spirit with a soul, living in a body. Because my deepest nature is now spirit, I am able to comprehend spiritual realities. The Holy Spirit energises our minds and hearts so that we can understand and experience relationship with God. 'For you did not receive a spirit that makes you a slave again to fear, but you received the Spirit of sonship. And by him we cry, "Abba, Father." *The Spirit himself testifies with our spirit that we are God's children*' (Romans 8:15–16, italics mine).

It is a profound spiritual truth that we weak and sinful people have been drawn into the relationship of the eternal Trinity. Father, Son and Holy Spirit have invited us into the love relationship that they have enjoyed from all eternity. What grace, what mystery! You and I have been lifted up to a position of honour and glory, children of God united to Christ by the Holy Spirit. The Trinity is not intended to be a remote theological truth, but the very source of our life and identity.

Now that our spirits are in union with God's Spirit, relationship and communication with God are the most natural things in the world. Our new nature is now the place within us to which God relates, and through which he makes himself known. Our rational minds lead us towards the knowledge of God, but it is our spirit nature that is able to have direct relationship with him. Because he has a place in us where he can rest and abide, intimacy with God becomes a reality as we learn to live according to our new spiritual nature. 'We have not received the spirit of the world but the Spirit who is from God, that we may understand what God has freely given us' (1 Corinthians 2:12).

After the resurrection, Luke writes, Jesus opened the minds of the disciples to understand the Scriptures (Luke 24:45). This is the work of the Spirit. Instead of the Word of God being a book of doctrinal information, it becomes the living Word of God to the believer, because his new spirit nature delights in its spiritual truth. The new nature is thirsty for the Word of God. We now have the mind of Christ (1 Corinthians 2:16). Without this new nature enabling us to perceive spiritual truth, we would be quite unable to participate in God's work on earth. Because we are now his friends and share his very nature, he delights to reveal his plans to us so that we may join him in the great work of redeeming a fallen world. We are now capable of being led by the Spirit, day by day and moment by moment. Just as a young child can take hold of his father's hand and be guided by him along the road, so we who are now spiritual beings can be guided in our spirits by our heavenly Father. 'Those who are led by the Spirit of God are sons of God' (Romans 8:14).

You are powerful

Standing on the boat in the middle of the lake, Jesus commanded the wind and the waves to be still – and they were. Walking in the desert, Satan came to tempt Jesus and thwart his mission on earth; Jesus resisted the temptations, rebuked the devil and sent him fleeing. Jesus was dead and buried, his life snuffed out. The cross had seemingly ended the final chapter of the life of the itinerant preacher from Galilee. But death was not strong enough to hold him, and the Son of God burst out of the tomb on the third day.

This same Jesus is at work within us. His power is available for every believer.

> I pray that the eyes of your heart may be enlightened in order that you may know the . . . incomparably great power for us who believe. That power is like the working of his mighty strength, which he exerted in Christ when he raised him from the dead and seated him at his right hand in the heavenly realms. (Ephesians 1:18–20)

Our new nature was created by an act of power that is comparable to the resurrection of Jesus from the dead. We who were dead are now alive, and we will never die again. Though our bodies may wear out and decay, our spirits will live for ever. God's resurrection power, which created our new natures, is constantly at work within us (Ephesians 3:20).

The presence of the life of Christ within us is the channel for God's creative and redemptive power to be released in us and through us. All the power that we need to live out this new life is already given to us. 'His divine power has given us everything we need for life and godliness, through our knowledge of him' (2 Peter 1:3).

It is already ours, now that we are in Christ. Can you believe this? Will you dare to look beyond your own weakness and begin to thank him that *everything you need for life and godliness* is already yours through Christ?

On 13 April 1970, Apollo 13 was launched from the Kennedy Space Center. En route for the moon, there was a complete failure of the instrumentation on the computer. The decision to abandon the moon landing was reluctantly made, and the primary goal was now to bring the astronauts safely home. Apollo 13 flew on into the moon's gravitational field and was pulled into its orbit. Using the moon's gravity as a kind of slingshot, the space capsule picked up speed. Then, just at the right moment, the booster rockets were fired and the spacecraft broke free from moon orbit and headed for home, finally landing in the Pacific on 17 April. Without the booster rockets giving them the power to break free from the moon's gravity, the crew would have continued to circle the moon until they all died.

In the same way, the flesh has the power to hold men and women in its grasp. Humanity does not have the ability to break free from the influence of sin and death. Just as gravity is a natural law that can only be overcome by a greater force, so sin and death are spiritual laws that can only be defeated by a greater power. That power is found in the person of the Holy Spirit. The power of the Spirit is the only hope for fallen humanity to break free from the old nature and live a new life that is pleasing to God.

'Through Christ Jesus the law [power, principle] of the Spirit of life set me free from the law [power, principle] of sin and death' (Romans 8:2). Christ has given us power to overcome sin. Our new nature, the spirit man within us, is capable of resisting any temptation and overcoming any sin. The fruits of the Spirit described in Galatians 5:22 are the manifestations of this power as it impacts our daily lives and creates within us the very character of Christ. Love, joy, peace, patience, goodness, kindness, faithfulness and self-control all find their origin in the person of Christ. Because he now dwells in you, his life and power are able to transform your very character. 'The Holy Spirit, indwelling a man, is capable of reviving the whole personality. Every faculty of man is to be developed and used to the glory of God who is saving man to the uttermost and who will bring to perfection the work he has begun!'[1]

Not I, but Christ

A story that made a great impression on me, and which helped me to understand the inherent power in being a new creation, concerns an event in the life of Augustine, the fourth-century church leader and writer. St Augustine grew up in Algeria, but moved to live in Milan. Young and rich, he discarded the Christian faith and indulged himself in a life of debauchery. He drank much and regularly visited the city's brothels. However, as a man of learning he became professor of rhetoric in Milan, and came under the ministry of Bishop Ambrose. Augustine started attending his sermons and slowly began to be intellectually convinced of the truth of Christianity, but baulked at the prospect of celibacy. Torn two ways, one day he ran into his garden and heard a child's voice cry out, 'Take up and read.' He sat on a bench, opened his copy of Paul's letters and read Romans 13:13–14: 'Clothe yourselves with the Lord Jesus Christ and do not think about how to gratify the desires of the sinful nature.'

Augustine later wrote, 'I did not want or need to read any

further. Instantly, as I finished the sentence, the light of confidence flooded into my heart and all the darkness of doubt vanished.' Not long after his conversion, Augustine found himself walking along one of the alleyways that he had frequented in his hedonistic days. From a window above him he heard the voice of a prostitute call out, 'Augustine, it is I, my love, it is I.' Lowering his head and pressing on, Augustine said to himself, 'Yes, but it is not I, it is not I.'

Though his physical appearance was still the same, Augustine knew that he was a new man. The old Augustine was dead and the new Augustine was alive. Living in the power of his new nature, he turned aside from the temptation and walked on.

Christ has given us power over Satan and all his attacks: 'The one who is in you is greater than the one who is in the world' (1 John 4:4). Jesus Christ has equipped us and enabled us to stand our ground in the spiritual battle because he himself is our strength. We have not been left alone to fend for ourselves: he now imparts his own strength and power to enable us to endure and withstand the very worst that Satan has to throw at us.

Even more importantly he gives us power to bring his blessing to the world. We are to be channels of his creative and life-giving power. The gifts of the Spirit are the manifestations of his life within us, and are the tools that we need to express the reality of Christ to an unbelieving generation (1 Corinthians 12). As we preach the gospel, heal the sick and love the poor, we will be living out the ministry of Jesus in word and deed, our new nature acting as a conduit of the redeeming power of God.

Humility or arrogance?

It is not easy to believe the truth about our new natures because most of us have learned to judge ourselves by our performance. If we are to embrace and enjoy our new natures, we must learn to see ourselves in a different way. Now that we are in Christ, we are not defined by our performance but by the work of God in us. If I sin, that does not mean that I am not holy; it means that I have not yet learned to live out and express my true nature. If I fail to live by faith and instead rely on my worldly understanding, it does not mean that I do not have the mind of Christ; it simply reveals that I have not yet learned to live according to my new identity. When I withdraw from the spiritual battle, feeling too weak to go on, it does not disprove the promise of God but shows that I have not learned how to draw on his power at work within me.

At these points of failure, the devil will be close at hand, seeking to lie to us and persuade us that we have not been transformed but only altered a little bit. This is a lie! You have been made holy, you have been given the mind of Christ and you have been given everything you need for life and godliness. In the next chapter we will look in more depth at the reasons we fail to live out the new life as completely as we might. But right now I urge you to look at yourself from God's perspective and acknowledge by faith and with simple trust that you have been changed and that you are a new creation in Christ.

It is a strange paradox that to believe that you have been transformed and raised to such an exalted level is in fact true humility! True humility is when we choose to agree with God. Humility means 'lowliness of mind' – in other words, when we lay aside our own point of view in deference to God's Word we are being humble. It is false humility to say of ourselves:

'It cannot be true. I am not worthy of such a high honour. I could not possibly think of myself as holy, or able to know the mind of God. Who am I to call myself powerful and filled with the very fullness of God? I sound so arrogant.'

None of us deserves this glorious gift from God, but it is true humility when we agree with God that this is what he has done in us, and then begin to live it out in our lives. We are called to rejoice, delight and be thankful for this work that has taken place in our lives, while always remembering where it came from. 'It is because of him [God the Father] that you are in Christ Jesus, who has become for us the wisdom of God – that is, our righteousness, holiness and redemption. Therefore, as it is written: "Let him who boasts boast in the Lord" ' (1 Corinthians 1:31).

To think that we had earned or deserved the gift of the new nature would be unbearably arrogant. It would reveal real deception in our hearts. Everything that we have comes from God, so let us boast in him and glory in his generosity and mercy.

Conviction of truth

It is crucial that we come to a place of conviction and understanding that we have this new nature, and that it is an objective reality that God has created within each one of us. If we are not settled in our own hearts and minds, we will either strive desperately to live our lives in Christ out of our own strength, or else we will resign ourselves to a standard that falls far short of God's best for us. 'Unless we know our inheritance as something already secured and settled in Christ and given to us by God, we have no foundation for going on.'[2]

James Hudson Taylor, one of the foremost missionaries in

the history of the church, pioneered the work of the gospel into the heart of China in the second half of the nineteenth century. But it was not until quite late in his life that he came into personal conviction of his union with Christ. He struggled so hard to be pure, but found himself failing continually and had nearly given up hope of overcoming his struggles. A letter from a friend came at a time of great turmoil; through it he received revelation from the Spirit.

> When my agony of soul was at its height, a sentence in a letter from dear McCarthy was used to remove the scales from my eyes, and the Spirit of God revealed the truth of our oneness with Jesus as I had never known it before . . . I saw not only that Jesus would never leave me, but that I was a member of his body, of his flesh and of his bones. The vine now I see is not the root merely, but all – root, stem, branches, twigs, leaves, fruit: and Jesus is not only that; he is soil, and sunshine, air and showers, and ten thousand times more than we have ever dreamed, wished or needed. Oh, the joy of seeing the truth! The sweetest part, if one may speak of one part being sweeter than another, is the *rest* which full identification with Christ brings. There is no fear that his resources will be unequal to the emergency! And his resources are mine, for he is mine and is with me and dwells in me. All this springs from the believer's oneness with Christ. And since Christ has thus dwelt in my heart through faith, how happy I have been![3]

We can live a life of intimacy with God, a life of joy, peace and freedom, only because of what he has done in us through the life-giving Holy Spirit. This is the basis of everything we do in the name of Christ. This is the work of transforming grace that he has accomplished in us. The essence of life is therefore *to become who you are in Christ.*

Lord Jesus, I thank you that you have come to dwell within me and have given me a new nature. Thank you that you have made me holy, spiritual and powerful. I choose to delight in my new identity. With your help I choose to turn away from pleasing my fleshly nature and dedicate myself to living according to the new person that I am in you. Amen.

EXERCISES

1. In what ways has your performance in life (success or failure) defined who you are?

2. In what ways do you struggle to see yourself as a 'new creation in Christ'? Read 2 Corinthians 5:16–18. Acknowledge those ways in which you see yourself in worldly terms, and pray that you will see yourself with God's eyes.

3. How do you react to thinking of yourself as holy? What is the basis for your holiness?

4. In what areas of your life do you most struggle to live in the power of God? Read 2 Peter 1:3–4 and claim it as a promise for these areas.

5. Rest in the truth of his completed work in you. Spend time thanking him for what he has done in you, irrespective of your feelings. Ask him to show you how he sees you, through his eyes of truth and love.

Part 2

HEALING THE WOUNDED SOUL

'May God himself, the God of peace, sanctify you through and through. May your whole spirit, soul and body be kept blameless at the coming of our Lord Jesus Christ. The one who calls you is faithful and he will do it.' (1 Thessalonians 5:23–4)

Part I

HEALING THE WOUNDED SOUL

4

Exposing the Strongholds

Andrew was gifted, popular and good-looking, yet he continually felt that he was useless and unattractive, and he found it hard to accept that other people genuinely liked him. Andrew had been a Christian for a number of years and in that time had received good biblical teaching at a thriving church. He simply could not understand why intimacy with God was not real to him, nor why he should struggle with feelings that constantly undermined his walk with Christ. He believed that Christ had come to bring him fullness of life, but that still seemed a long way off.

As we prayed and talked, details of his life began to come out that revealed the root of the problem. As a child he had grown up in a family that played a lot of tennis. His parents and three older brothers were excellent players, but Andrew was a rather chubby and uncoordinated child. He did not make the same progress as his brothers and was therefore seen as something of a failure within the family. Sadly, his parents did not encourage him in those things at which he was gifted, so from an early age he felt he was second-rate and let the family down. To make matters worse, his father stopped coaching him and instead invested his time and energy in the other brothers. Andrew remembered feeling inadequate, foolish, stupid and ashamed.

Like all children, Andrew believed that what his parents were communicating was the truth about himself, and began to behave in ways that reflected this. He began to protect himself from the pain of repeated failure by withdrawing into himself and refusing to try to achieve at anything. He made few friends and kept his own company. Because of his behaviour he failed at school, and his peers made little attempt to befriend him because of his aloofness.

This pattern of behaviour continued through his teenage years and into early adulthood, when he came to know Christ in a real and personal way. As he encountered the truth of Christ's love for him, he began to change, and grew in confidence and an understanding of his value in God's eyes. But after a period of initial change, his spiritual life began to stagnate and he struggled to relate to God as a loving heavenly Father who treasured him as a wonderful son. However much he strove to believe the truth with his mind, he still felt lonely, inadequate and ashamed.

Andrew is like so many of us. Having started a genuine relationship with Christ and having made real progress in the initial year or two, we find that the old fears and feelings return to undermine us. If we have received such an incredible inheritance from Christ, as the Scriptures reveal, why can we not live in the fullness of it? Why do we still struggle to enjoy intimacy with God and to live mature and authentic lives?

The battle with the flesh

> So I say, live by the Spirit, and you will not gratify the desires of the sinful nature. For the sinful nature desires what is contrary to the Spirit, and the Spirit what is contrary to the sinful nature. They are in conflict with each other, so that you do not do what you want. (Galatians 5:16–17)

Paul uses 'the sinful nature' (Greek *sarx*) to describe those thoughts, attitudes, emotions and desires that oppose the way of the Spirit. This is the false self created by, and accustomed to, living in alienation to the redeeming power of Christ. Before the fall, in their state of innocence, Adam and Eve did not know alienation from God and therefore their desires were pure, their thinking was true and their wills were straight and upright. They lived permanently out of the true self in union with the life of God. At that time they had no old nature or false self, but through the fall they were separated from this state of complete union with God and their souls became distorted by the absence of his presence. Sin and evil are the results of man's fall from innocence, the direct result of our alienation from the source of all truth and light.

In Figure 4, each cross represents those thoughts and attitudes, feelings and desires that are yet to be brought into captivity to the truth. We battle with them daily and long to be free of their influence. While our new nature is perfect in Christ, its influence over the totality of our thinking, our emotions and our choices is not yet complete. When we obey the desires of our old nature, it does not mean that our new nature has been tarnished or that we have become less holy in the eyes of God. We sin out of our old nature but because God relates to us as new creations, we know that 'there is no condemnation for those who are in Christ Jesus' (Romans 8:1). The old

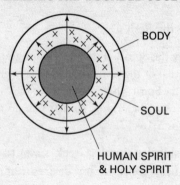

Figure 4 – The Holy Spirit within

nature brings every human under the destructive power of sin and death, but the work of the Spirit in us redeems and restores our souls so that we can live life fully under his direction and power.

As the Spirit of God flows into us, he encounters the results of the years of obedience to and identification with the old nature. Our souls have been damaged, wounded and twisted because of our participation in sin. All sin finds its ultimate origin in the devil, who is the source of all rebellion against God, and it was his deception that led to the fall of Adam and Eve. Satans work was defined by Jesus: 'The thief comes only to steal and kill and destroy' (John 10:10).

The nature of sin is to participate in the work of destruction that Satan has been perpetrating since the creation of mankind. Whenever we have followed the desires of our old nature, which is our false self, we have wounded God, wounded our neighbour and wounded ourselves. Our attempts to bring order and meaning to life have been the attempts of fallen men and women to handle life in a fallen world, but instead of bringing life they have sown death and destruction. Paul describes some of the acts of the flesh in his letter to the Galatians: 'The acts of the sinful nature are obvious: sexual immorality, impurity and debauchery; idolatry and witchcraft; hatred, discord, jealousy, fits of rage, selfish ambition, dissensions, factions and envy; drunkenness, orgies and the like' (Galatians 5:19–21).

This is not an exhaustive list of the acts of the sinful nature, but it describes attitudes and desires that are common to all people. Without the life of Christ indwelling us and enabling us to live in his strength and with his values, we will always live according to the old nature.

Identity in the old nature

None of us can ignore the reality of the false self in our lives. However, the degree to which it has a hold over us depends on the degree to which we have constructed a sense of our own identity around sinful attitudes and behaviour. We all have a profound need to feel that we are valuable, that we belong and that we are significant and gifted. These are the three pillars of emotional health and are critical to the development of a healthy identity and self-esteem.[1]

Value

We need to know that we are special, valuable and of infinite importance simply because we exist and not because we have had to earn or prove it. With this sense of value we can take our place in life as a precious and beautiful creation whose inherent worth is beyond question. Without it we feel that we are not worthy of the love and attention of others, and we either fight to prove ourselves or withdraw from relationships or challenges.

Belonging

We need to know that we belong, that we are secure in our own identity. Someone who knows this deep sense of inner security is able to feel at home in themselves even in threatening situations. Without it, we constantly feel the need to find a place that is safe, and even when we get there we still feel insecure, anxious and ill at ease.

Significance

We were each created for a purpose, with gifts and talents given to fulfil our unique destiny. If I know that I am capable and gifted, that I have been created well, then I will naturally want to express myself and use the skills that I possess. When that self-knowledge is missing, there is a deep-seated sense of inadequacy within us that either prevents us from achieving or causes us to strive to prove ourselves.

The impact of the fall

The creation narrative in Genesis reveals that Adam and Eve were created with inherent value, purpose and security. The knowledge of their value and worth was found in their love relationship with God. They were made in his image and walked and talked with him in the garden. Their value was imparted to them by the love and attention that God paid them. They did not know what it was like to feel worthless or unwanted. Their purpose was to tend the creation in which God had put them. As his representatives on earth, they knew that they had a unique calling and purpose (Genesis 1:26–9). In this place of utter contentment their identities were secure because they knew that they belonged, that they were valuable and were significant in God's purposes for the creation.

This ideal state was utterly devastated by the fall. Man and woman fell from the state of being God-conscious to being self-conscious. Experiencing separation guilt and loneliness, they began to develop an identity that was separate from the one they had known in Eden.

We are their children. We too have sought to establish our identities apart from the grace of God. We have tried to recover that which was lost at the fall through our sinful, weak and twisted ways. The desire in us for value, belonging and significance is God-given, but our attempts to meet these valid needs have been rooted in our own wisdom and strength. Once we understand that we have built our identity on the desires and choices of the old nature, then we will begin to understand why it is that we find some sins harder to be rid of than others. It is very hard to give up the old ways that have given us a sense of our own identity, even if those ways have been destructive and unhealthy. Andrew had to begin to learn what it meant to find his sense of value, belonging and significance in the love, acceptance and purposes of Christ. As the Holy Spirit was at work, he began to see that what underpinned his way of life was not faith and trust in God, but fear and anxiety stemming from the damage that others had inflicted on his life by their words and actions.

Wherever we are struggling to overcome sinful attitudes and behaviour patterns, we will find that they embody to some degree our sense of value, significance and belonging. They give us meaning, and our old nature does not want to let go of them without a fight.

Strongholds in our lives

Outside Corinth stood an imposing fortress, built as a stronghold to garrison soldiers and armoury. It is likely that Paul had this stronghold in mind when he wrote to the Corinthians:

> For though we live in the world, we do not wage war as the world does. The weapons we fight with are not the weapons of the world. On the contrary, they have divine power to *demolish strongholds*. We demolish arguments and every pretension that sets itself up against the knowledge of God, and we take captive every thought to make it obedient to Christ. (2 Corinthians 10:3–5, italics mine)

The uses of the concept of strongholds in Christian literature today are many and varied. However, Paul is quite explicit about what it means: strongholds are arguments and pretensions (literally, 'high things') that set themselves up to resist the knowledge of God in the life of a person. Strongholds can therefore be defined as any thought pattern, attitude, idea or concept that is resistant to the advances of the knowledge of God.

Paul uses the language of warfare to convey how seriously he takes the presence of strongholds in the lives of Christians. He uses terms such as war, fight, weapons, demolish, captives. He is not prepared to take lightly the presence of these destructive attitudes in our lives, knowing that when they are present in us they will resist a deeper knowledge of God and are access points for Satan to influence us to oppose God's will.

Where do strongholds come from?

Cultural strongholds

As we grow up within a culture we will unconsciously take on board the mindset of the day. Within a fallen society this mindset will involve some presuppositions that will conform to God's truth and others, maybe most, that will not. A child born in the 1960s in the communist USSR would have grown up with the belief system that God did not exist. It was compulsory to teach and to believe in 'scientific atheism', and consequently the mindset of the culture acted as a stronghold against the knowledge of God. I heard a speaker say that 'Western society suffers from truth decay'. Relativism, the belief that there is no absolute truth, is a stronghold in our culture today. To proclaim that Christ is THE truth is seen as arrogant and intolerant in an age when enlightenment is seen as an acceptance of the truth found in all religions. Cultural strongholds are accepted by the people of a society except where individuals or organisations vigorously oppose and expose the false mindset.

Family strongholds

Families can have their own particular mindset which will be passed on to the children with little or no resistance. David grew up in a family that set great store on financial success and hard work. His father continually taught the children that nothing in life comes free and that you have to work to earn every penny. When David came to know Christ, he found it very difficult to receive the free grace of God and to trust that Christ could meet his every need. He thought it was his job to earn whatever God wanted to give him. He had learned to understand life through the mindset of his family. It gave him identity and meaning, but it opposed the knowledge of God's grace and mercy.

Personal strongholds

'I know God loves me, but I cannot get rid of a nagging fear that I may be abandoned by him if I am not a good enough Christian.'

'I know I am forgiven, but however hard I try to believe the Scriptures, I find I am constantly feeling guilty and trying to earn my forgiveness. I can't seem to stop it.'

'I believe that God will provide for me, and I know that I shouldn't worry, but I always feel so anxious and don't seem to be able to rest in his love.'

'I want to be pure, but I am constantly assailed by lustful desires and images.'

Most of us know what it is like to believe something in our heads but not experience the reality of it in our hearts. It is often said that the truth needs to drop the six inches from our heads to our hearts. This experience is common to most of us, because our souls are damaged and a split has occurred between the rational and cognitive way of thinking of the head and the symbolic and intuitive way that the heart understands. The head may believe one thing while the heart may believe something entirely different, and so we find that we are not able to walk in the confident certainty and power that truth releases when it is established in both the head and the heart.

My own experience and the stories that people regularly share with me as a pastor reveal that for most believers there are areas in which they continually struggle to have victory, with little or no success. Feelings of lust, fear, hopelessness and anxiety, compulsive desires and emotions, thoughts of self-rejection and self-hatred, insecurity and inadequacy – we all have to deal with these destructive thoughts and feelings from time to time, but in many of us they are a continual source of guilt, failure and shame.

When we recognise an area in our lives that stubbornly resists bowing to God's truth and rejects knowledge of him, then we need to ask God to show us the nature of the stronghold and its reason for being present in the first place. David's stronghold developed as he was taught to live according to the values of his family. Andrew's stronghold began as a response to the pain that he suffered in his family. His parents' love was inadequate and conditional, and in order to cope with the agony of rejection he began to build a wall to defend himself. The wall grew higher and thicker with every action and experience that reinforced the belief his parents fostered in him that he was foolish, inadequate and pathetic.

Strongholds that have a grip on our personal lives develop because we find in them something that brings us some measure of value or security. For Andrew, his stronghold gave him some element of protection. In his heart he felt he had little value and even less ability, but at least he felt he had found a way of protecting himself. The only problem was that by the time he had become an adult his walls of protection had turned into a prison that he could not break free from. In fact he could not even see anything wrong with it, until the Holy Spirit showed him that his whole identity was based not on God's love and truth but on his own warped experience of life. The church he attended did not understand that his condition needed healing. Instead, they gave him more scriptures and urged him to try harder and have more faith. Sadly, this only served to reinforce his sense of failure and did nothing to heal the deep wounds that were in his heart.

A stronghold develops in this way when the initial emotional wounding is compounded by the belief that the rejection, criticism, abandonment, abuse or other damaging experience was deserved. We then begin to live in ways that reflect our now distorted view of ourselves.

Pictorially our strongholds can be represented like this:

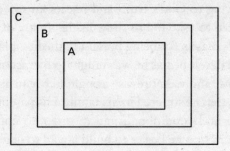

Figure 5 – Strongholds

The initial pain (a) is compounded by the belief system (b), which in turn is reinforced by the behaviour and habit patterns (c). Together, these create a formidable protection that is designed to help us survive and to establish some form of personal identity. This is why strongholds are so damaging: they are our human attempts to cope with life and they resist the healing and redeeming grace of God.

Very often our unseen strongholds are affirmed by the church culture to which we belong. Competitiveness, people-pleasing, self-sufficiency and striving for success are a few of the behaviour patterns that influence us and which are often seen as acceptable within church cultures. When personal strongholds conform to the mindset of a church it is hard even to perceive the need to break free from them.

Head and heart

If biblical truth is only learned in the mind then we may have the appearance of understanding, but when we encounter a situation that tests the reality of our faith, the deeper heart knowledge will undermine and generally overcome the rational concepts of the intellect. 'As a man *thinketh in his heart* so he is' (Proverbs 23:27 KJV, italics mine). Jesus taught that 'From within, out of *men's hearts*, come evil *thoughts*' (Mark 7:21, italics mine).

If the truth sits in the head but has not been established in the heart, we will experience a gap between what we believe to be true and our ability to live in that truth. When we have rational knowledge of the truth but cannot live in the power of that truth, then there is likely to be a stronghold in the heart. We may have the appearance of wisdom and maturity that intellectual knowledge gives but lack the deep-seated heart knowledge that brings reality to the theories.

Andrew knew the Scriptures well, but the imagery in his heart was sabotaging his attempts to put it into practice. He believed in his head that God was a loving Father, but whenever he sought to come close to him his heart knew that fathers were demanding and that their love was conditional and caused pain. Consequently, his heart shut down to protect itself. Though Andrew was doing all the things he had been taught in church, he simply could not find the love and intimacy that everyone else seemed to be enjoying. His heart needed to be healed and restored. The intellectual truths that he had learned sat like a thin film of paint over a rotten and damaged old table. On the surface he appeared fine and could join in the best of theological debates, but his heart had utterly failed to grasp the reality of the truths he assented to in his mind. The table looked fine but was in fact in danger of collapsing.

We might assume that we would always want to demolish the strongholds in our lives, but this is not always the case. Where there is a stronghold, it is there for a very good reason. We have built it in order to find protection in an unsafe and threatening world. Andrew found it very hard to allow Christ to begin to demolish his stronghold, because over the years it had become part of his identity. To have to start trusting people again, to allow them to get to know the real Andrew, was very threatening. Not only that, but he was not even sure he knew who he was. Now that Christ was telling him he was not a failure or inadequate or foolish, Andrew hardly knew what to do with such knowledge. He had to learn to let go of his old identity, one that felt secure but was in fact destructive, and embrace a new identity that was being imparted to him by God.

The process of dismantling a stronghold is a painful one and requires us to trust Christ to a new and deeper level. It is when we feel naked, vulnerable and defenceless that we have the opportunity of encountering the Lord in a deeper and more substantial way. It is only when we get to the end of ourselves that we truly begin to find God.

Repentance and healing

In his book *Man's Search for Meaning*, Victor Frankl writes about his fellow prisoners in Dachau, the Nazi concentration camp:

> Some of the prisoners who had longed for freedom, and who had lived in captivity for many years, found freedom hard to take. When they were eventually released they walked out into the sunlight, blinked nervously and then slowly and silently walked back into the familiar darkness of the prisons to which they had become accustomed for such a long time.[2]

Both repentance and healing need to take place in our lives if we are to walk out of our strongholds and allow the Holy

Spirit to lead us into freedom; but dare we take the risk that change always brings?

In our society, healing is a more popular term than repentance. This is partly because we have thrown off the belief in a higher authority to whom we are responsible, and therefore see no need to turn away from any course of action or style of living. Our desires are seen as the only authority to be obeyed. If it feels good, do it. The aim is not to live lives that are obedient to a higher and transcendent truth, but to live lives that are happy. Happiness is the god our society serves. We therefore look for healing to make us happy but often resist repentance because it challenges our selfish desires for fulfilment.

There is no true healing without true repentance. Repentance is the process by which we turn away from our false identity and embrace our true one. By dying to the old we are able to embrace the new. No longer choosing the independent and self-centred ways, we become dependent on God in true humility. We choose to live no longer in the destructive patterns that have brought us a sense, albeit false and superficial, of our own value, security and significance, and we choose to live and think in ways that conform to the life-giving truth of Christ. We seek our identity in him. His love enables us to know that we are valuable, that we belong and that we have a unique contribution to make to his work on earth.

> I have set before you life and death, blessings and curses. Now choose life, so that you and your children may live. (Deuteronomy 30:19)

Every day we have the choice to choose life or to choose death. Every thought that we think, every word that we speak, every feeling that we obey, is a participation in either life or death. What we think, speak and do will reflect whether we are living according to the principle of life or the power of death. Now that we are in Christ, we have the capability to choose life every time, but will we do so in practice? In order to turn away from our old identity, we must know what to turn towards. Jesus' fundamental message was: 'Repent and *believe the good news*!' (Mark 1:15, italics mine).

For many, the experience of repentance has been empty and powerless. Having no realisation of what they are to turn towards, they turn away from their sin on one day, but fall back into it all too soon because there was nothing to take its place. The gap that was created in their life was not filled and therefore the old problem returned or was replaced by a new form of compulsion. Instead of the wonderful release and freedom that accompanies true Spirit-inspired repentance, the person is left in a state of confusion and discouragement. The old and destructive identity in the flesh must be replaced by a new and transforming identity in the love and friendship of the Father, Son and Holy Spirit.

Demolishing strongholds

The source of the stronghold that is rooted in pain, as Andrew's was, must be healed but this is impossible if there is no repentance.

Don't confuse repentance with sadness. Sadness and disappointment, without a genuine determination to change, are simply a form of self-pity. We may weep tears of disappointment or feel ashamed that we have not lived up to our own standards, but these are not repentance. Repentance is the determination to turn from the evil that we have participated in.

The real person will never emerge until he chooses to walk free from the grave clothes of the old self. The Holy Spirit will not violate your free will. Until we choose to hand over the keys to our strongholds the Lord can only sit outside, weeping as he watches us damage ourselves through our twisted and sinful attempts to manage our lives according to our own wisdom and effort.

Imagine a man holding a snake that keeps biting him. There is little that the doctor can do until the man throws the snake away and offers his wounds to be healed. The healing described in the later chapters can only come as we run to Christ for life, and in doing so forsake the old thoughts, feelings and attitudes that we have held on to. Your stronghold only has as much power as you give it. Choose to abandon it and to find your true identity in Christ, and the life-giving Spirit will begin the work of demolition and healing that we need so much.

Let no one tell you that this is not a painful process, because that would be a lie. A part of you has to die. We have to put to death the old, false and compulsive ways of living, and the meaning we found in them. But as we live the way of the Spirit and refuse to compromise with the old nature, we will begin to allow God access to the deep-seated causes of the destructive thoughts and behaviour patterns in our lives. Only then can he truly heal us.

Lord Jesus, I choose to invite you to reveal to me any strongholds that are present in me. I choose to let you into my stronghold to demolish it. Please forgive me for seeking to establish an identity separate from you. I turn away from it and look to find my meaning, value and purpose in your love. I am willing to let my old identity die so that you can create in me a new, lasting and life-giving identity that is born of the Spirit. Thank you, Lord. Amen.

EXERCISES

1. What aspects of the 'sinful nature' do you struggle to over-come?

2. In what areas of your life are you aware of a split between head knowledge and heart knowledge?

3. Are you aware of the presence of any stronghold in your life that resists your attempts to change it?

   In what way does this stronghold give you a sense of value, belonging or significance?

   What is the source of the stronghold?

4. What would it mean for you to repent of this stronghold?

   In what ways would it be painful for you to allow this stronghold to be demolished?

5

Foundations for Real Change

The breakthrough in Andrew's life came when he realised that the way in which he had been coping was not merely unhelpful, but sinful and resistant to the work of the Spirit within him. Because he had an honest heart and a keen desire to live fully for Christ, Andrew confessed his sin to the Lord and we invited the Holy Spirit to come and begin the work of healing in his heart. As we prayed, Andrew clearly recalled a memory from his childhood and saw himself standing forlorn and rejected at the local tennis club. He was on his own while his father and mother were training his brothers. This memory symbolised all the pain, rejection and shame that was stored up in his heart and which had been motivating him since childhood.

Tears began to flow as the hurt, loneliness and shame came to the surface. We kept praying, seeking the Lord for a deep healing of the scars and wounds in his heart. By this time Andrew was deeply engaged in the memory, and we invited Jesus to enter it and reveal his love for Andrew. Afterwards Andrew told us what happened next. He saw Jesus walk across the tennis court and pass by his family, with eyes of love fixed upon him. Taking him by the hand, Jesus led Andrew away from the tennis club and they went for a walk together, where they spent time talking and playing.

In that moment, Jesus imparted to Andrew's heart – and to his mind – the truth Andrew had found so impossible to believe. Jesus loved him! The images that the Holy Spirit was revealing to Andrew's heart (remember that the heart thinks primarily in images and feelings) were the vehicles for him to be able to receive the truth.

Think of the symbolism of the images. Jesus walked past the people who had always been the 'important' and 'successful' ones and instead came to meet Andrew. This showed the deep value that Christ set on him, and began to heal the rejection that he had felt from others. Second, Jesus had taken hold of his hands and led him away from the tennis club, which spoke to him of receiving a new identity from Christ, one that was no longer dependent on his family's approval. Third, the time and attention that Jesus had given him imparted a deep sense of love and value to Andrew's heart, thereby beginning the work of restoring his self-esteem.

This encounter with Christ took place in his imagination, and began the process of disentangling the twisted imagery present in his heart. From that moment on he began to see himself as Christ saw him, and was able to live with new strength and determination. The change was not complete by a long way, but a deep work of healing had been started. He began to know in his heart that he was truly loved and precious in the eyes of the Lord. The scriptures that spoke of the love of God as Father no longer seemed so theoretical but carried the reality of their meaning into his heart. Coming out of his shell, the real Andrew began to grow and be seen as the man that God had made him to be.

From self-image to God-image

All of us have images of ourselves that are stored in our hearts. According to my dictionary, an image is 'a mental picture, idea or conception'. We can measure our height, describe our hair colour, reveal our exam results and give all sorts of facts about ourselves, but it is our mental picture or conception of ourselves that will determine whether we live healthy or unhealthy lives. Do you see yourself as beautiful or ugly, wanted or rejected, gifted or inadequate? Most of us have a mixture of images of ourselves, some of which are enabling and some which are disabling. In my own life I have had some good, healthy and solid conceptions of myself. As a teenager I was successful at golf and through it found a sense of value and competence that kept me going during some very rough times. On the other hand, I have continually struggled with a profound sense of inadequacy and worthlessness which I sought to cover up with an arrogant public-school image. At times I was able to believe my own facade, but in my darker moments these deep-seated feelings would rush to the surface and leave me struggling with their impact.

The way we live is directly related to the image that we have of ourselves, and most particularly in the three areas that we have touched on already: value, belonging and significance. Each of us needs to make the journey from seeing ourselves through the lens of our own experience to seeing ourselves through the lens of God's perfect truth. God knows you utterly and completely. His perception of you is not twisted or limited in any way. He knows your strengths and your limitations, he knows your personality and your gifts. He understands what you love to do, and the way in which you love to do it. He sees the real you and is longing to call you up and out of the limited and twisted image you have of yourself. As we begin to perceive ourselves in the light of God's perfect truth, we are no longer dominated by the words and actions of those people in our past who have shaped us and caused us to see ourselves as we do today.

Josh McDowell expressed this truth when he wrote: 'A healthy self-image is seeing yourself as God sees you, no more and no less.'[1]

God sees you with his perfect insight. He sees all you were created to be, and he is intent on fulfilling in you all the potential that he has put within you. It was this same prophetic insight that enabled God to speak to Gideon and call him a mighty warrior. God saw it in the Spirit; as Gideon responded in faith, so the reality came into being and Gideon became a great leader. Jesus called Peter a rock, though he was still a weak and fearful man who would even come to deny his Lord. As Jesus spoke truth into Peter's life, the power of his word began to change and develop Peter into the man that Christ had made him to be.

The same process needs to take place in our lives. We need to allow Christ to rename us and call us into our new identity, but to begin with we need to recognise what has happened in our lives to give us the image of ourselves that we have today.

Love tanks

I first came across the concept of 'love tanks' in Dr Ross Campbell's book, *How to Really Love Your Child*.[2] It was a revelation to me that has significantly changed my whole approach to parenting, to ministering healing in the power of the Holy Spirit and to counselling hurting people. What are love tanks? Imagine for a moment that every child has a heart that is like an emotional tank. This emotional tank needs filling with love by the parents, because no child has the capacity to fill it on their own. Every child has a God-given need for loving touch, focused attention and words of blessing. These are every bit as vital as the child's physical needs for food, drink and warmth, and must be given if the child is to develop a healthy self-esteem. If the love tanks of little Jenny are full, she will feel good about herself and behave in ways that will maximise her gifts and potential. Feeling that she is a valuable and precious person, she will naturally believe that she can make friends and succeed by using her abilities which have been blessed and affirmed by her parents.

Now you may be asking what this has to do with our self-image. The key to it is this: the degree to which your love tank was filled with a knowledge of your own value, belonging and significance will have determined the fundamental nature of your self-image. A child who has had his love tanks continually filled through his early life – the first seven years are the critical ones – will develop into an adult who has a healthy view of himself and who is less likely to develop a web of destructive thought patterns and attitudes. I have met people who are not Christians but who are psychologically more healthy than many of the Christians that I meet day by day. They may not know Christ, but they are well balanced, creative and gifted, and are able to form committed, faithful and intimate relationships. Why? Because in their formative years they received the empowering love of parents that enabled them to grow and develop in healthy ways. When such a person receives Christ and is regenerated by the Spirit, they are likely to find it easier to enter into an intimate relationship with Christ and to express the true self than those who have not experienced the same healthy upbringing. Those whose love tanks were insufficiently filled are likely to struggle with many compulsions, addictions and desires that stem from their childhood.

Knowing who we are

Our capacity to know who we are is imparted to us by our parents. When we are born we do not have an in-built knowledge of our own selfhood. We are like a blank sheet of paper, waiting to be drawn on. Our genetic inheritance determines our personality and physique, but how these basic building blocks for life are developed is dependent upon the way our parents shape them and bless them. In the same way, we are born with a capacity to know and receive love and affirmation, and the degree to which it is imparted will determine the extent to which we will be able to give and receive love. A child who has her love tanks filled will have a heart that is like a ripe and juicy grape, but the child who has little love and worth imparted to her will have a heart like a dry and shrivelled raisin. In one the capacity to live a full life is greatly enhanced, but in the other potential is limited and the heart will be crying out for the unmet love needs to be satisfied. That is why a person whose love tank has never been adequately filled will find themselves struggling with compulsions and desires that war against their attempts to live out the Christian life. A full and healthy love tank is vital to a full and healthy life.

As we look now at how our love tanks are filled, and the impact on us if they are not, may I encourage you to read with one eye on the information itself, and the other eye on the state of your own love tanks.

A sense of belonging

Each of us has a deep and primal need to feel that we belong, that we have a place in this world that is ours and ours alone. When I know this, I feel deeply rooted and secure in my own being. This is not pride or self-sufficiency but in fact the very opposite, and is in itself a safeguard against those two destructive and sinful attitudes of the heart. At its deepest level this sense of belonging and security is found in the mother's love.

At the time I am writing this, there is an advertising campaign that uses a picture of a baby in the womb, with the caption 'The safest place you have ever been in'. This is a great truth: the womb was intended to be the place where we are formed in utter safety and peace. God's ideal was that every child would be wanted and received by their parents with delight and joy, and that as they grew in the womb they would intuitively know that they were safe and secure. Sadly, this is not always the case and recent research shows an increasing understanding of the impact of the formative months in the womb. The womb is the first place in which we learn whether life is safe or threatening, and whether we are wanted or not. Deep healing needs to take place in those who have experienced trauma or rejection in the womb.

The first thing that the child needs, having come through the trauma of birth, is to be held in the arms of the mother and to begin the bonding process by feeding at her breast. This is a crucial stage, as the child's first experience of life outside the womb needs to be positive and nurturing. In these early hours, days and months, the child is receiving his first – and therefore most formative – experiences of life in the world. If the infant is enabled to bond well with the mother and to know the deep peace of being held close to her heart and satisfied by her breasts, then the deep sense of belonging so crucial to our lives will be set into his heart. According to the Miami Medical Schools Touch Research Institute, premature babies who received three fifteen-minute periods of slow, firm massage each day showed a 47 per cent greater weight gain than other children in the same ward who did not receive the same attention. These same babies showed improved sleep, alertness and activity.[3]

Separation anxiety

The child who is separated from his mother for any significant length of time within the first two to three years, or who is unable to bond effectively with the mother, may suffer from 'separation anxiety'. This is a condition that leaves the child, and later the adult, with a deep-seated sense of aloneness, anxiety and restlessness. Those who suffer from it speak of always looking for a place to feel safe and wanted, while others feel that they are always afraid of death and are unable to trust themselves to another for fear of abandonment. Some feel it physically as a gap or a hole within them that has always been there, a sense of non-being.

It is a popular misconception that because the baby or child cannot verbalise the fear or pain she may be experiencing, then she will not be affected by it. Often people say, 'She is just a child; she will grow out of it. It won't harm her.' In fact the reverse is true. It is exactly because the child has no way of rationalising or contextualising the pain that she is utterly defenceless to wounding. The actions or words spoken over her go straight to her heart and establish themselves in her inner being. The infant cannot say to herself, 'I know Mummy is very tired or sick right now, but I know she loves me and wants me and is ready to hold me and protect me, so I will be a good little baby and simply wait till Mummy is ready to love me again.' What in fact happens is that the child feels deeply abandoned, lost and fearful that she will die because she is separated from the source of her life, her mother. These feelings are then too painful to bear and are split off from the conscious mind and deeply repressed, but they still profoundly influence the attitudes and feelings of the child as she grows.

This condition of separation anxiety can be caused in a baby as well as in a small child by a lack of bonding to the mother or by a period of enforced separation from her arms. I can think of a little boy who hated to let his mother out of his sight; we traced the root of the anxiety back to the holiday that the parents took when the boy was eighteen months old. Separation anxiety needs healing by a deep work of the Holy Spirit, because it will undergird any other compulsions that are born out of this deep-seated fear of being abandoned, deserted and unwanted. (A note to concerned parents at this point: there are no neat formulas concerning separation anxiety. If you have left your child for a significant period it does not automatically follow that he has separation anxiety. The only way of telling is by observing his behaviour and by the discernment of the Holy Spirit. Healing is possible, as will be seen in Chapter 7.)

The sense of belonging needs to be imparted throughout the child's formative years and on into adolescence. Physical touch is crucial to this, and no child can get too much appropriate physical affection from his parents. Hugs and kisses, cuddles and tickling, rough and tumble, a reassuring hand on a shoulder, big arms that comfort a child in pain or simply holding hands in the park – these and many others are all forms of intimate and affirming physical touch. Physical touch imparts a sense of value to a child by communicating in a non-verbal way that the child's presence is valuable and special. It will also continue the process of imparting the sense of belonging that is so crucial to healthy development.

There is great potential for harm when a child is punished physically but not affirmed physically. This happens all too often when fathers seek to discipline their children, but have never learned to show them physical love as well. Impartation of this sense of security may begin in the mother's womb and at her breast, but the father's role is extremely important as the child grows and learns that he is not an extension of the mother's body, but a separate creation with an identity in his own right.

The concept of 'appropriate physical touch' is crucial. A teenage boy emerging into adulthood needs a different expression of touch than a small boy going to school for the first time. When physical touch is given that breaks the boundaries of the individual's own sense of privacy, or when the physical touch is used to meet the parent's own need for love and affirmation, then it becomes suffocating and destructive. Sexual abuse is one form of inappropriate touch, but so also is a goodbye kiss when demanded by an insecure parent who needs the reassurance themselves. Parental love can become smothering and it can suffocate the child or young adult in their attempt to gain independence from the parents.

It is quite common to find that those people who have never had enough physical touch as children crave to be held and nurtured as adults. It is also not unusual for adults to shy away from physical touch because they have experienced it as a manipulative tool in the hands of their parents. As God heals our hearts, he will fill our love tanks with the touch of the Holy Spirit and will make up for the touch deficiency, or abuse, that we may have experienced in our lives.

Underneath are the everlasting arms. (Deuteronomy 33:27)

For I am convinced that neither death nor life . . . nor anything else in all creation will be able to separate us from the love of God. (Romans 8:38)

When this healing is imparted, it enables us to enjoy the sense of belonging and the 'at home' feeling that is so central to a healthy person.

A sense of value

Just as God made us to know that we belong to him and are safe in his arms, so too he made us to know that we are of infinite worth to him: 'You are precious and honoured in my sight' (Isaiah 43:4).

When we come to know Christ, however, we may not easily be able to enjoy the deep heartfelt knowledge of our value and worth in his sight. God does not make junk, and you are not a second-rate creation that God made on a tired Friday night! You may have been hurt and damaged over the years, you may have lived out of strongholds that destroyed your self-respect and the respect of others, but you still have inherent value and worth before God. The more we understand the horror of the death of Christ and the agony he endured for each of us, the more we will grasp the value that he places on our lives. The depth of his suffering reveals the height of our value to God.

However, our ability to take hold of this truth is greatly affected by the degree to which our parents filled our love tanks with a sense of value. It is important to state again that children do not know their own value as they grow up; this must be given by the parents. This needs saying again and again, because we tend to assume that it is our own fault if we did not grow up with full love tanks. A child will always assume that his parents are right and that he is wrong. It is always the parent's role to be the one who blesses the child – not the other way round.

How should our love tank have been filled with value? Every child needs to be noticed, to be accepted for the person that he or she is. It is only as our parents stepped out of their adult world into our childish world, took notice of us and accepted us, that our worth and value was discovered. Unconditional acceptance must be imparted through focused attention. The extent to which your parents made you a priority in their lives, and spent time doing the things that you enjoyed and encouraging you in them, will have given you a sense of your own unique value.

Chris has an abiding memory of his childhood. He recalls walking alongside his father, who was cutting the grass on a drivable lawn mower. He remembers calling out to his father to get his attention, but the noise and his father's determination to complete the job meant that he never noticed his son, who was longing to spend time with his dad. That memory was symbolic of his childhood; the adults had their own plans and the children were expected to fit around them. No one spent time focusing on Chris's own needs or desires, and through their actions they communicated the sorry truth that to them the boy was not important. We need to have time and attention poured into our lives as we are growing up. We need to hear that we are incredibly valuable, and not for any other reason than simply that we exist. After I had finished encouraging a young and highly gifted woman, she cried out from her heart, 'Don't affirm me for what I do, affirm me for who I am!' Starved of the life-giving blessing of unconditional acceptance, she craved this deep affirmation that did not depend on the success of her actions.

If I have not known the deep and rich affirmation that is rooted in unconditional acceptance and pure delight in my existence, then I will be frightened to be myself. I will not even know who 'I' really am if I have not known that I am valuable. This is why we have run to our strongholds and developed a false identity. Very often our false identity is made in the image of our parents, who told us what we should be in order to be valuable. Long after we should have found our own adult identity, we are still living in a childish and immature identity that seeks to be told that it has value and worth.

A sense of significance

Every child needs an enormous amount of encouragement. It is the affirmation of our gifts, talents and personality that enables us to dare to reveal who we really are, and which imparts to us the sense that we can make an impact in this world. The following gives us an insight into the early life of King Edward VIII, who abdicated the throne in 1936.

'Every Friday the teacher took me to my father's room. "And what has my son learnt this week, Mr Hansell?" the King asked. And the answer was always: "Not very much, I'm afraid, Sir. Edward does not like his lessons. He never listens to what I say."

'When Mr Hansell left the room, my father was angry with me. "What's wrong with you, child?" he said. "Are you stupid? Why can't you learn anything?"

"But the lessons are so boring, Sir," I replied. "And Mr Hansell hits me."

"I don't understand you, Edward. You're a baby. You're so weak. You'll never be a good king. A king must be strong. Go to your room and stay there until morning."'

'I spent many days alone in my room,' Edward wrote later. 'I never played with other children and I didn't have any friends. I lived in the most beautiful house in England but I was always lonely and sad. I saw my mother once a day at dinner-time and I saw my father three or four times a week, but they never gave me any love. I was afraid of them and everything I did was wrong.'[4]

When we are discouraged by criticism, we retreat from life and the good within us remains hidden from view. When someone sees in me that which is beautiful and good and affirms it, then it begins to come forth and be established in my life. I cannot know that I am competent, gifted or capable unless someone whom I respect tells me so. It is our parents' words of affirmation that will fill the love tanks in our hearts with a sense of our own significance and ability.

All too often, words of criticism and discouragement are used to keep a child in his place. Cruel nicknames can be particularly devastating to a child's self-esteem as he grows. Time does not heal the power of destructive words spoken into a child's life; the old words must be replaced by the blessing of the heavenly Father, who is always ready to encourage and affirm his listening children.

If a sense of significance is lacking, then we will struggle to believe that we can make a difference or that God could use us. Very often a strong person will be utterly determined to prove that they can 'make it in life', and to show everyone that they are gifted and therefore valuable and worthy of respect. God has made each of us with gifts and talents that are to be used to fulfil our own unique calling in life, 'for we are God's workmanship, created in Christ Jesus to do good works, which God prepared in advance for us to do' (Ephesians 2:10).

No one else can do the good works he has prepared for you to do, and you are not called to fulfil anyone else's calling either. Knowing that we are his workmanship, his priceless work of art, will enable us to work without striving, perform without competition and achieve without fear of failure.

Stop now and reflect on the last few pages. In the 'tank' printed below, draw in the level at which you personally feel (a) safe, secure and at home in yourself; (b) valuable, special and precious; (c) competent, gifted and capable.

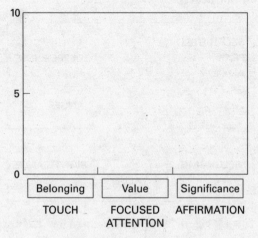

Figure 6 – Our love tank

Unhealthy emotions

If our love tanks have not been filled with good emotions, then the space that is left unfilled will not remain empty. It will contain damaging and negative emotions that will spill over into our lives. Imagine that little Jenny has had her love tanks filled to level 5 out of a maximum of 10. The remaining emotional capacity will be filled with emotions that will reflect the negative experiences that she had as a child. Just like the rest of us, she will have her own particular mix of healthy and unhealthy emotions, because we have all grown up in a fallen world. No parents are perfect and no environment is perfect, so we must learn to recognise the source of those negative emotions that underlie our strongholds and contribute to our sinful behaviour. These emotions cannot be healed if we will not face them or consider where they may have come from in the first place. The diagram below shows the sort of emotions that can fill our hearts.

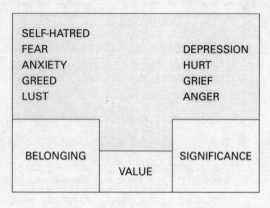

Figure 7 – Emotions stored up

The emotions that are stored in our hearts will either support or resist our attempts to develop an intimate relationship with Christ and with our spouses, children and friends. If there is deep anxiety we will find it hard to trust. If there is shame, we will find it hard to be open and vulnerable. If there is false guilt, we will find it hard to enjoy the freedom of knowing Christ's complete forgiveness.

Not all emotional or mental wounding finds its roots in childhood. We can be deeply damaged as adults and healthy childhood foundations can be rocked by traumatic experiences in later life. However, these damaging events are generally easier to recognise than those in childhood, and are also normally easier to heal because their impact is not so deeply felt as in those formative years. All negative and damaging actions and words need healing, in order for our hearts to be free from emotions that undermine our call to live in intimate relationship with Christ.

SPIRITUAL MATURITY AND EMOTIONAL WHOLENESS
GO HAND IN HAND.

YOU CANNOT BE SPIRITUALLY MATURE
IF YOU ARE NOT EMOTIONALLY HEALTHY.

I hope that by now these two statements are obvious, and that you are increasingly aware of the impact that your emotional health has on your relationship with Christ and your ability to enjoy all the riches that he has given you. Negative emotions that are rooted in our past will always lead to strongholds in our lives, which is why each of us needs to begin the journey to wholeness and to face the past and its impact, both positive and negative, on our lives. The next two chapters reveal the steps that we can take to move towards wholeness and the healing of our hearts.

Father God, I ask that you would reveal the true state of my heart to me. I desire that my heart be free from the presence of unhealthy and negative emotions that prevent me from embracing a deeply intimate and fulfilling relationship with you. Please teach me to see myself through your eyes and to know that I am immensely valuable to you, that I am secure in your love and that you have made me with gifts and talents that are able to bring glory to you. Thank you that

*I am your beloved child, and that you are my perfect parent.
Amen.*

1. Describe how your parents did or did not:
   (a) touch you in ways that made you feel safe, secure and loved;
   (b) spend time with you and make you feel valuable and special;
   (c) speak words of encouragement and blessing, and so give you a sense of your own competence and ability.

2. What positive emotions have been present in your love tank, and how has this affected your life so far?

   What negative emotions have been present in your love tank, and how have they affected your life so far?

3. Are there other experiences outside your childhood that have had a significant impact, both positive and negative, on the way you view yourself?

4. Consider how you view yourself. Take time to describe your self-image and consider how it affects your relationship with God and other people.

6

Walking into Freedom

Standing in the middle of Epping Forest, I felt bewildered, hurt and angry. Even harder to bear, my pride had been dented. My wife Ceri and I had gone for a walk in the local woods, but our relaxed chat had turned into something much more profound. I found myself listening to Ceri as she very graciously began to express how frustrated she was feeling in our marriage. I prided myself in being an open, generous and thoughtful husband, but the picture she was painting portrayed a lack of emotional intimacy and heart-to-heart communication between us. As I asked her to explain where I was failing her, she spoke of how I 'shut down' emotionally when I found things difficult, leaving her isolated and unsupported. She described my lack of sensitivity to the needs of her own heart, and how out of touch I was with my own emotions.

This was not what I wanted to hear! However, it was this conversation with Ceri that first caused me to stop and consider that perhaps I was not quite the man I believed myself to be. Maybe I was not as whole as I had thought.

I could not deny how Ceri felt, as she spoke with great insight and grace. Therefore I was faced with a choice. Either

I could belittle her needs as 'merely those of a woman', or I could swallow my male pride and begin to face my own lack of emotional health. Looking back to that day, I marvel now at the way I failed to see my own personal brokenness and also the way I had learned to pass it off as 'normal'. At the time I was genuinely unaware of my own protection system and the way it blinded me to the deeper issues that lay beneath. I was in a place of deep denial, and quite unaware of it.

If we are to begin to walk into the freedom that Christ has in store for us, then each of us needs to begin to address the root causes of the broken and destructive behaviour in our lives that damages our relationship with God and one another. There are some key steps that we need to take.

Ask for the Holy Spirit's help

After our conversation in the woods, I found myself asking the Holy Spirit to reveal what was really going on within me. Mine was a simple and heartfelt prayer that echoed the cry of David:

> Search me, O God, and know my heart;
>   test me and know my anxious thoughts.
> See if there is any offensive way in me,
>   and lead me in the way everlasting. (Psalm 139:23–4)

As we turn away from justifying ourselves and our actions, and dare to ask the Lord to show us what is going on in our hearts and in the unseen place of our motives, he will send the Holy Spirit to be our counsellor and the revealer of truth (John 14:16–17). The Spirit will be gracious and tender, but also persistent and truthful. God has the perfect plan for healing and restoring us, but it is his plan and in his time. We cannot cope with too much reality at any one time. I could not have coped with seeing at one moment all the brokenness that was gradually to be revealed over the next few years. As I look back over the healing work that God has done in me, I can clearly see that he has done it at just the right time and in just the right way, though I may not have felt so at the time!

Looking to Christ

It is crucial to fix our eyes on Christ and not to go looking for the problems and wounds of the past. We look first to Christ and invite the Holy Spirit to bring to the surface whatever emotions or attitudes are hidden beneath our consciousness. It is God's work to 'bubble up' these things, and not our job to find them. Only in this way will we be kept from introspection and an unhealthy obsession with our own needs and wants.

Choose to face the truth

Each of us needs to be prepared to see the things that we may have spent years, even decades, learning to suppress and hide from sight. We need to face the truth that the Spirit is showing us about ourselves, our families and the events that have shaped us into being the people we are today. This is primarily a choice of the will that decides to put truth above our own comfort. In this way we take personal responsibility for our lives and our actions and are kept from blaming others for our own sinful behaviour.

I first met Jeremy when he came to see me about his feelings of inadequacy and rejection. As we talked I was struck by his determination to face up to truth. He was prepared to acknowledge the root causes of his unhealthy feelings and to own responsibility for his behaviour. Stephen, on the other hand, beset by similar feelings and struggles, continually sought to evade his own responsibility and, while saying he wanted to be whole, sabotaged the process by not facing up to the truth about himself. Jeremy is now forming healthy relationships and being used by God in evangelism; Stephen, unfortunately, is still stuck in his old attitudes and feelings, and has made little or no progress.

Unless we choose to see what the Holy Spirit wants to show us, and take seriously our own personal responsibility to change, we will remain where we are. Like an old record we will get stuck and go on living in the pain, repeating the same patterns of behaviour that never lead to freedom. It is not easy to see the truth about ourselves, and we struggle to acknowledge the truth for various reasons.

Our desire to be in control

Where we have hidden our diseased attitudes and emotions, we will be afraid to have them revealed lest we lose the control over them that has given us a sense of safety and order. One woman expressed the fear of relinquishing her control system when she confessed, 'If I faced my pain, it would be like popping the cork out of a champagne bottle. It is too dangerous and too messy to do that.'

A city businessman described it well when he said, 'I have put a steel cap on the oil well within my own heart, but the pressure is building and building and I am frightened to let go.'

This is a painful place to be in, and all of us will find ourselves in it at some point in our lives. The only way out is to go forward! It is scary to let go of our control systems, to walk out of our strongholds, but God will heal us only with our permission and full cooperation.

To give him lordship of our inner pain is a testing step, but one that reveals the reality of our trust in him. Something within our hearts cries out, 'Will he shame me as others have done before?' 'Will he really heal me or will I be disappointed once again?' 'Can I dare to trust my heart to him when I feel so fragile and vulnerable?' We will never know until we dare to turn and trust him.

Though he is the Lord of heaven and earth, he is also tender, faithful and full of grace. Let these words from Isaiah sink deep into your heart, releasing faith within you as they do so:

> Here is my servant, whom I uphold,
>   my chosen one in whom I delight;
> I will put my Spirit on him
>   *and he will bring justice to the nations.*
> *He will not shout or cry out,*
>   *or raise his voice in the streets.*
> *A bruised reed he will not break,*
>   *and a smouldering wick he will not snuff out.*
>   (Isaiah 42:1–3, italics mine)

He who brings justice to the nations is awesome in power and majesty, yet in his mercy he will not crush the weak and the needy. To give him control of our emotions is the step of faith at the centre of Christ's healing work in us. There is no way round it: everyone who seeks to be made complete in Christ must take this step by handing over control of their hearts to the Lord. He will not fail us, for he is true to his word and he has promised to 'complete the good work he began in you' (Philippians 1:6).

Running from our own pain

When God brings up our pain and the wounded emotions within our hearts, a part of us wants to push them away or ignore them. They hurt! We rush into activity, turn on the TV, go to the pub or simply refuse to recognise them. However, we cannot say goodbye to something until we have first said hello to it! Years of learning to repress such feelings need to be unlearned. This is a choice we must make, however painful. There are no quick fixes, no magic words and no shortcuts. Facing our inner pain may well feel like 'walking through the valley of the shadow of death', but we must determine to do it.

Most of our lives are characterised by the desire to protect ourselves from pain or inconvenience. Endless advertisements promise freedom from the struggles of life and offer a quick route to peace and comfort. From chocolate bars to health insurance, from credit cards to lawnmowers, products are offered to make life more comfortable. The path to wholeness is one that goes directly against our desire for personal ease. If we are to find wholeness in Christ, we must choose to walk into the very pain that we have done our best to escape.

False loyalty to parents

When I first met David he was unemotional, cold and distant. He was driven at work and while he could meet the material needs of his wife and young children, he failed to meet their emotional ones. When asked about his relationship with his mother and father, he replied instantly: 'My parents are wonderful. There is absolutely no way this has anything to do with them.'

David is typical of most of us. We find it very hard to look objectively at our own childhood, and there is a part of us that cannot bear to think that our parents could be partially responsible for the pain we now feel as adults. Over the ensuing weeks David began to look more closely at his relationship with his parents. Though it was painful for him to accept, he saw for himself how needy and manipulative his mother was, and how distant and unaffirming was his father.

Most of us grow up assuming that our childhood was great, our family was normal and nothing we are struggling with today has anything to do with our parents.

In Chapter 5 we saw how parents must communicate their love if a child is to be able to receive it and grow up with a healthy self-image and sense of value and worth. It is therefore vital that we are able to understand and face those areas where our own parents failed to meet our genuine and appropriate needs. This means acknowledging the ways in which we were hurt because of their words and actions, and where we were hurt by a *lack* of the right words and actions. Harsh and unkind words leave us with emotional 'wounds', but a lack of touch time and blessing leaves us with emotional 'holes'. Both are destructive, but the 'holes' are often much harder to discern.

If we are to grow up and leave the past behind us, we have to begin to recognise those things about our parents which were good and those things which were not. This will enable us to get to the roots of many of the struggles for peace, security, value and worth that we face day by day. It is a very painful but a very courageous step to take when we are prepared to ask God to show us the truth about our childhood. The 'child' within us still is frightened of facing the truth, but as adults we still have to choose to confront the reality of the past. Invite God to show you in what ways your parents blessed you as a child, and in what ways they failed to bless you. Until we begin to unravel the past and disentangle the fact from the fiction, any growth or change in our lives will be limited, and we will still be motivated by many hidden desires and emotions.

Honouring your mother and father

'My parents would feel so betrayed if they knew how I felt!' cried a woman who was beginning to admit what she really felt towards them. One of her fears of expressing her true feelings was that she would be disobeying the command to 'honour your father and your mother' (Exodus 20:12). When we face the truth about our parents, we are not dishonouring them. It is only when we use that truth to manipulate them or damage their reputations that we begin to dishonour them. Most of the time our fear of dishonouring them is because we are admitting to ourselves things that we have not dared face for years. We may feel we are betraying the people who brought us up and who gave us life in the first place, but we are not. What we are doing is recognising their fallibility as people. Failing to break this false loyalty to the myth of perfect parents will leave us in a place in which our growth to maturity will fall far short of God's very best for us.

Learn to express your emotions

Driving home one evening, I was in turmoil. On the one hand I had shut down my emotions and distanced myself from Ceri because of something that had taken place earlier in the day. On the other hand I could feel a deep frustration rising within me. I tried very hard to shut it all off, but it would not go away.

'You're angry, aren't you?' Ceri said, trying to make contact with a husband who had disappeared into an emotional black hole.

'No, I'm just frustrated,' I calmly replied.

'I think you're angry.'

'I am *not* angry.' This time my voice began to rise.

'Are you sure?'

'I AM NOT ANGRY!' I shouted, immediately realising that my attempts to call it 'frustration' had failed miserably.

I was not frustrated – I was angry. Anger was an emotion that I had never known what to do with. In order to be good, I had shut it away in a locked room somewhere inside me lest it emerge to embarrass me. The best I could do was to euphemistically label it 'frustration'; now, for the first time, I was having to admit to myself that I did indeed have feelings of anger.

As I began to give God permission to reveal my heart to me, I started to see things I did not like very much. It was like the loosening up of a heavy chest cold as the Holy Spirit began to get beneath my superficial control and bring to the surface my hidden emotions. I wanted to get well, but I did not know what to do with all the phlegm!

Deep within our hearts are many emotions that need to rise to the level of our consciousness. Freedom from emotions such as anger, bitterness, grief, shame, fear, loneliness, insecurity and inadequacy means letting them up and out! These are the negative emotions in our love tanks that undermine our growth to spiritual and emotional maturity. If we do not express them, then it will be as if we were holding a beach ball under water. Soon it will escape our control and burst to the surface.

Very often, when praying for someone who has pushed down and suppressed their emotions, I start by asking them to give the Lord permission to open their hearts and reveal their true feelings. This is a bit like the opening of a tightly packed sardine tin! While the lid is on, God does not have permission to move deep within our hearts. Although keeping the lid on our emotions may stop the painful emotions 'coming out', it also stops the Lord's love 'coming in', and this will result in a reduced capacity to know him from the heart. Once the person gives the Lord freedom to bring these wounded emotions into the light of his love, then progress is sure to begin.

In order to be released from damaged emotions we first need to learn to express them. As we do so we may even find ourselves revisiting the memory of the events that we have done our best to forget. Human beings are very good recorders. We have a remarkable capacity to remember and store away the feelings, experiences and thoughts that we have throughout our lives. I have seen and heard a grown man cry with the sounds of a tiny baby, as the Spirit touched a place of deep childhood pain within him. Such experiences give credence to the view that all our experiences of life, good and bad, are recorded and stored within us. My eldest son put it well when he once described a past event that had caused him pain as a 'memory hurt'. All of us carry around memory hurts that need expressing before they can be released from the body's memory banks.

Emotions are physical

It helps us to express our emotions once we understand that they are physical in their nature and not disembodied and ethereal. Emotions are feelings, and feelings are felt in the body.

Have you ever felt sick with worry? When you are anxious, do you feel your muscles tense, especially in the shoulder region? Have you ever seen someone go red with anger or embarrassment? How do you respond when you are sad? Do you weep real, wet, salty tears? Do you feel heavy, and does your countenance reflect your sadness? These things take place because emotions are physical in their nature.

The Scriptures bear this truth out. In the Gospels Jesus is

described as being moved with compassion (Matthew 9:36, 14:14, 15:32, 18:27, 20:34). The Greek word used to describe his compassion is *splanchizomai*, which has been graphically translated as 'moved towards one's innards' and 'moved in the intestines, entrails or bowels'. The Greek word traces the source of the emotion to the body organs where they are felt. Jesus' compassion came from the depths of his very being. Similarly, one of the most common words for anger is *choleo*, which refers to the feeling of 'gall or bile' (we get the word 'choleric' from it). Anger is very physical. Because emotions are so physical in their nature, they need to be expressed physically too if we are to be healed and cleansed of them by the Holy Spirit.

A little earlier I mentioned the lady who was fearful of facing her pain because she knew it would be messy, and therefore she preferred to keep the cork in the bottle. In one respect she was quite right: expressing the damaged and painful emotions that the Spirit reveals in our hearts can be a messy business. There may be times when we will need to weep, to feel again the loneliness that may be within us and which gnaws at our insides. Feelings of grief may cry out from within us. I well remember one of my best friends coming to terms with the grief of never really knowing his own father. In a time of ministry, when we were praying God's richest blessings on him, he started to weep and cry out, 'Daddy, where were you? Daddy, where were you when I needed you?' In that moment he was expressing all the grief of having an emotionally absent dad. His pain was all too real but was being wonderfully healed as he looked to his heavenly Father in the midst of it. It certainly was messy, but it was the doorway to restoration, healing and a deeper walk with his Lord.

This aspect of the healing process is easier for some than for others. If you

- have spent your life being a 'good child';
- have been taught that to express unhealthy emotions is wrong, sinful and unchristian;
- have learned to deny your real emotions by internalising them.

then daring to express your pain and anger may well be hard for you to do at first. Sinful, wounded and damaged emotions will not go away if we deny them hard enough. Repentance does not mean repressing them, but rather admitting them, expressing them before God, and then allowing his Holy Spirit to forgive, cleanse and heal the emotions that we long to be free from. God wants us to be real with our emotions and to stop pretending.

I would suggest that you do not tell your parents, or anyone else who may have caused you pain, until you have worked through your feelings and come out on the other side. Only then will you be able to talk about the issue objectively. We need to begin to express our emotions in a place that will not damage others, yet which still enables us to be real. A close trusted friend, a church leader or a counsellor may provide excellent opportunities to be honest, real, safe and accepted. Most of the emotions that arise can be dealt with on our own with God, but companions can be particularly helpful if we cannot face the pain alone.

Writing letters that we never intend to send, hitting our bed, acting out our anger in private, shouting, yelling or painting our emotions, all are ways of helping to express emotions that need releasing. Each of us needs to find forms of expression that work well for us, remembering that what is helpful for one person may not be helpful for another.

Getting real with God

As a 'good boy' I found it hard to verbalise and express what I considered bad emotions, and as an adult – and a clergyman to boot – I found it even harder! I was greatly helped as I saw how David handled his own emotions in the Psalms. David, one of the greatest men of God in the Bible, gets angry; he weeps, shouts with rage, is quiet, wails, moans, gets frustrated and impatient, feels hopeless and quite often appears depressed. All this from David, King of Israel and writer of the Word of God.

> My thoughts *trouble me and I am distraught*
>   at the voice of the enemy,
>   at the stares of the wicked;
> for they bring down *suffering* upon me
>   and revile me in their anger.
> My *heart is in anguish within me;*
>   *the terrors of death assail me.*
> *Fear and trembling have beset me* . . .
> I said, 'Oh, that I had the wings of a dove!
>   I would fly away and be at rest. (Psalm 55:2–6, italics mine)

See also Psalms 28:2–4; 22:1–2; 6; 42:1–5; 73:1–3; 102:1–2.

As we read the Psalms, we read the outpourings of the hearts and souls of very real and earthy people. David and the other psalmists bring their real emotions into the presence of their God. How unlike most of us, who so quickly put on an attitude of deep spirituality, thinking that somehow God would be offended to know what we were really thinking and feeling. Learning to be real with God is a vital step towards a deep and intimate relationship with him. God knows our hearts better than we do, and I believe he is both saddened and, to some degree, offended when we try to be something that we are not. Expressing our real emotions to God does not mean wallowing in them; rather it means being honest with him in the midst of our struggles.

Intimacy through honesty – journalling

The psalms of David are an expression of the living relationship that David was developing with his God. A journal is one very helpful way of following David's example. It is not a diary of the events and facts of life, but is one way in which we are able to pour out our hearts to God. We write out our darkest feelings as well as our purest, our fears as well as our hopes, and are forced to face the reality of what we are going through. It stops us evading the issues and challenges that God is setting before us, and is enormously helpful in enabling us to recognise what the Lord is seeking to do in our lives.

The first time I kept a journal I failed miserably. I was guarded in what I wrote in case some day it should be published. (Oh, the pride in my heart!) I was also trying to be profound and spiritual, not realising that a journal is a place to write out the good and the bad. Before too long I gave up because it was so boring and superficial!

Through the encouragement of other older and wiser Christians I began journalling again. This time it was not on a daily basis but only when I had something that I needed to express in order to acknowledge what was going on within me. I learned to write out my emotions and my thoughts. Sometimes it was praise and thanks, sometimes a thought on a passage of Scripture or a promise that I was going to hold on to. At other times it was the struggle I was encountering with sinful and damaged emotions such as insecurity, lust or anger. Having learned to shut down my heart in the past, I was now consciously acknowledging its existence and influence on my life. In this way my heart began to thaw and repressed and frozen emotions began to emerge. I began to learn the language of the heart, not just of the head. My relationship with Jesus began to get much more real.

Often when I am struggling with destructive emotions I begin to journal, and as I do so I begin to see more of what is going on within my heart. I then talk to the Lord about it. As I do, I often get revelation of the reasons for the pain, and I turn to him for healing and restoration. In this way I aim to turn my journal into a dialogue, in which I listen for his healing word to me after I have first expressed my wounded heart to him. Here are some helpful hints on journalling:

1. Write whatever you want in your journal. There are no 'shoulds' or 'oughts'.
2. Write the good and the bad. Resist all attempts to sanitise your words. Do not condemn yourself (Romans 8:1).
3. Use your journal to push back your boundaries of honesty, openness and vulnerability.
4. Seek to make your journal a two-way dialogue. Learn to listen for God's word to you. Learn not to censor the good things God begins to say to you, even if you find them hard to receive.
5. Find a trusted friend with whom you can begin to share your journal.

Journalling comes more easily to some than to others. I am an activist and find it hard to stop and reflect. While I find it difficult to give adequate time to journalling, I value it immensely when I do.

Learning to pour out our hearts to God is essential if we are to develop the intimacy with him that we are seeking (1

Samuel 1:15; Psalms 42:4, 62:8). God is frustrated with us when we appear squeaky-clean and sanitised. The path to intimacy and wholeness is not neat and tidy. He is looking for men and women who will develop a walk with him that is real, honest and earthy.

Again and again, David and the psalmists would hear from God and receive a fresh revelation of his love for them after they had first been truly honest with him. In the same way the Prodigal Son came to know the reality of his father's love in the midst of an earthy, smelly but wonderfully passionate embrace. The elder brother never entered such a place of intimacy and love with his father, because he had never looked for such a hug. His life was too clean and tidy, too legalistic and pure, to recognise his own need for intimacy. In just the same way, the sinful woman in Luke chapter 7 pushed back the boundaries of common decency, only to find Jesus loving and accepting in response. She came far closer to Jesus than the Pharisees, who remained aloof, distant and satisfied with their own piety. Our brokenness provides us with a glorious opportunity to reach a place of great intimacy with Christ. The wounds of our pain can become the marks of tender intimacy.

Each of the steps outlined in this chapter is crucial in the process of opening us up to the healing work of the Spirit of God. We will look at this further in the next chapter, but before we move on you may want to pray this prayer with me:

Father God, I ask you to send your Holy Spirit deep into my heart. With your help, I choose to see whatever you reveal to me about myself, my childhood and my past. I dare to face the truth, however painful. I give you control of my heart and emotions. Please give me the grace to express my wounded and painful emotions to you. I look to you for hope, and trust that in your presence I will find acceptance and healing. Thank you, Father God. Amen.

EXERCISES

1. In pursuing emotional wholeness as an integral part of maturity, are you more likely to deny your real feelings or to become self-absorbed and introspective?

2. How do you feel about acknowledging your parents' weaknesses and failings?

3. What negative emotions do you find it hard to express? What makes it hard for you to express them?

4. What is your response to the idea of starting a journal that is real and earthy?

7

The Healing Power of Christ

Allowing our hearts to express all the emotions stored within them is often painful, but it is a critical step towards wholeness. While we are unable to choose which emotions need to be faced – that is the work of the Holy Spirit – we can choose what we are going to do when they surface. What we choose to do with the unhealthy emotions and attitudes that bubble up into our consciousness is every bit as important as allowing them to be revealed in the first place.

The presence of the will

Every day we make choices, and the quality of the choices that we make plays a significant role in determining the life that we live. I make small choices all the time: for instance, I choose what to wear, what to drink or what to watch on the TV. But other choices have a greater impact, and a choice made in a split second can alter the course of a whole life. Our ability to choose and to exercise free will is at the core of what it means to be human and to have been made in the image of God.

We have minds that think primarily in rational and logical

terms, we have hearts that think in an intuitive, symbolic and emotional language, but we also possess a will. It is the will that determines what I do with the thoughts and feelings that flood my being throughout the day. It is my will that chooses how I live and therefore it is a deeper and more powerful principle than either the mind or the heart.

In Deuteronomy chapter 30, God calls the Israelites together and speaks to them about the future and the choices that they will make:

> This day I call heaven and earth as witnesses against you that I have set before you life and death, blessings and curses. *Now choose life*, so that you and your children may live and that you may love the Lord your God, listen to his voice and hold fast to him. For the Lord is your life, and he will give you many years in the land he swore to give to your fathers. (Deuteronomy 30:19–20, italics mine)

Every day we make choices that will cause us to participate in either life or death. The degree to which I enter into the life that Christ has won for me will depend upon the commitment I make with my will to choose life in each and every situation that I encounter.

The state of the will

James was an underachiever. He rarely initiated anything and was blown along by the events that happened around him. While in prayer he saw himself sitting on a roundabout as the cars circled him, quite content to watch the world go by. James had a passive will, maybe even a broken will. Years of domination by his mother and a history of discouragement had left him fearful of initiating lest he fail and prove again how worthless he felt he was.

Sarah struggled with anorexia over a number of years. She possessed a powerful will, but one that was operating in the wrong direction. The will was turned against herself, and with great determination she was literally choosing death day by day as she refused to eat.

Jenny has an eager will, but one that lacks strength. She is excited by the prospect of change and growth, but when she encounters the pain and struggle that always accompanies the journey to maturity, she withdraws and consoles herself with the thought that it isn't the right time, and that she will wait until she feels stronger. Because her will is so weak, she invariably falls at the first hurdle despite her good intentions.

Brian has a controlled will that exerts great discipline over his life, his actions and his emotions. He feels the need to be in control of every situation in which he finds himself, and he chooses to minimise any inner discomfort by over-controlling his emotions. As a Christian he is knowledgeable, unflappable and efficient, but he lacks intimacy or spontaneity in his relationships because his emotions are suppressed.

These are all examples of different ways in which the will can be operating destructively in Christians – people who believe in Christ, but who are choosing 'death' in ways that are preventing them from walking in freedom and maturity.

Using the will perfectly

In Jesus we see the will operating perfectly. His head, his heart and his will are working in unison. They are all aligned to truth and there is no separation within his own being. He is literally the complete man, and therefore even in the greatest times of testing his will is submitted to the purposes of the

Father. In each and every situation, Jesus chooses life and so walks in the freedom of perfect obedience.

The greatest test of his will was in the Garden of Gethsemane, and it is this incident that gives us a model of how to deal with emotional and mental pain.

> He withdrew about a stone's throw beyond them, knelt down and prayed, 'Father, if you are willing, take this cup from me; yet not my will, but yours be done.' And being in anguish, he prayed more earnestly, and his sweat was like drops of blood falling to the ground. (Luke 22:41–4)

This was the supreme moment of temptation for Jesus. His mind was searching for an alternative way to bring about our redemption without the horror of the cross. His emotions were screaming with pain at the prospect, and such was his agony that his sweat was like drops of blood. In the midst of this turmoil, it was with his will that Jesus chose to walk in obedience to the Father. Despite the pressure exerted on him, Jesus refused to allow his mind or his emotions to rule him, but instead used his will to keep them in harmony with the purposes of God. This refusal to be separated from the Father's will, in rebellious isolation, is the perfect model of the use of the will. When we choose with our will to align our lives with the will of God, then the will has the power to bring those wounded and damaged parts of our soul into the presence of God, and there find restoration and healing.

In the midst of our own temptation, pain and suffering, we too must operate out of a deeper place than our minds or our emotions. We must choose with our wills to stay in the place of pain and to wait for his enabling grace to heal and restore us. Years of practice have taught us to cope by using sinful and destructive behaviour patterns that have established strongholds in our lives. As we begin to take our thoughts captive to Christ, as we allow the Holy Spirit access to the core of the stronghold and as we develop a vision of how to live and react in godly and healthy ways, then it is our wills that will execute the plan. If we do not choose to live in truth, then we will only perpetuate the sin and resist the healing and sanctifying work of the Spirit.

Standing in the pain

In his book *Setting Love in Order,* Mario Bergner describes his journey out of a homosexual lifestyle to wholeness in Christ. On one particular weekend he faced severe emotional pain and temptation, and as he describes the experience, we see a true and godly use of his will. One Thursday afternoon Mario discovered that his lectures for Friday had been cancelled and therefore he faced three nights and two full days before he would meet with fellow believers for prayer and support at church. In that time he was determined to resist the temptation to escape the loneliness that he dreaded by returning to his old haunts, and the sexual encounters that he had used for so long to ease the pain in his heart. On Thursday evening he was fine, but by Friday morning deep anxiety and overwhelming temptation gripped him from the moment he awoke. His whole body was consumed with desire.

> Aligning my will with God's will and deciding that a sexual fall was out of the question, I took a Band-Aid and placed it over the inside of my front door. Then I promised God that I would not break the seal until Sunday morning came, no matter how anxious or sexually tempted I became.

The temptation grew worse on Friday, and by Saturday Mario had done all the chores he could think of to take his mind off the struggle. Finally, with no distractions left to him, he consciously turned to God, and in the midst of his severe trial he came before the cross and sought the help of the Lord.

> Better to be before the cross, than to end up alone and hopeless. The words of Job 13:15 rang in my ears. 'Though he slay me, yet will I hope in him.' Even if my present temptations never let up, I would stand before the cross and hurt till kingdom come if necessary. Unable to form my prayer, my anxious and painful loneliness became my prayer. There in the midst of unbearable suffering, I resolutely decided to obey God. That is exactly what God was waiting for me to do.[1]

As we seek to be healed of the wounds of the past, we will encounter times of great agony of soul and will feel intensely alone and vulnerable. Like Mario, we must refuse to go back the way we have come. We must choose to press onwards into life and leave the old sinful ways of numbing our pain and inner fear. Like Pilgrim in Bunyan's classic, we must stick our fingers in our ears and refuse to listen to those voices that call us back to the ways of the old nature, and we must run forward, crying out, 'LIFE, LIFE!'

Before the cross

In the depth of our own personal struggles and temptations to act out of the old nature and to live according to the ways of the false self, we must come before the cross and hurt. It is at the foot of the cross that we can most clearly see the Suffering Servant. At the cross we encounter him who has entered into our deepest suffering and who now hurts with us. The eternal God has known what it is to experience agony, trauma, loneliness and utter despair. The cry of Jesus on the cross: 'My God, my God, why have you forsaken me?' has been echoed down the centuries by men and women who have lost sight of their God under the burden of intense agony. Because he, the Lord of life, has uttered such a cry, it gives dignity to all those who feel abandoned and alone.

Standing before the cross we identify with Christ, prizing truth and purity above false comfort and capitulation to the power of the lie. In doing this we allow the power of the atonement to become a living reality in our hearts.

As we look upon the cross, not only do we identify with Christ's act of wilful obedience, but he identifies with our sorrows and pain. 'Surely he took up our infirmities and carried our sorrows' (Isaiah 53:4). As we come to him in simple faith, not only is the debt of our sin cancelled but the consequences of sin are also dealt with. On the cross Christ took into himself, into his physical body, all our wounded, diseased and sick emotions, and brought them into the work of atonement which brings peace and wholeness to mankind.

'He himself bore our sins in his body on the tree, so that we might die to sins and live for righteousness; by his wounds you have been healed' (1 Peter 2:24). The Hebrew understanding of man was that he was an integrated creation. Body, soul and spirit were all inextricably linked. Salvation and wholeness were therefore synonymous; consider Jesus' words in John 7:23 (italics mine): 'Why are you angry with me for *healing the whole man* on the Sabbath?'

It is at the cross that the supernatural reality of God's healing power takes place. The 'healing work' is not in itself the difficult thing. The difficult thing, for both God and ourselves, is getting us to a place where we come to Christ open, raw and vulnerable. God has to allow us to be exposed to the reality of our personal brokenness in order for us to be truly healed.

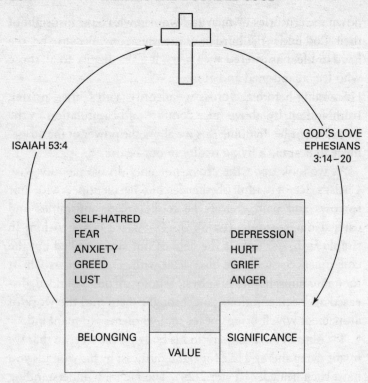

Figure 8 – Healing the whole man

Releasing the power of forgiveness

In order to appropriate the full extent of the forgiveness and healing that Christ bought for us once and for all upon the cross, we too must release forgiveness to those that have sinned against us. In the Lord's Prayer, Jesus revealed that it is only as we forgive that forgiveness is released to us: 'Forgive us our debts, as we also have forgiven our debtors.'

As we seek to be released from the impact of words and actions that have damaged us in the past, we will need to learn how to forgive those who are the very reason for our present pain. Forgiveness does not come easily or naturally to us; we have to learn how to do it.

Huddled in her chair, Rachel whispered, 'I can't forgive him, I simply can't do it.'

'Rachel, what is it that you are trying to do when you forgive?' I asked.

'I can't love him, and I won't pretend it never happened.'

Rachel's concept of forgiveness was one that was so far from the truth that it rendered her incapable of forgiving the man who had so grievously wounded her.

Forgiveness is NOT:

- pretending that it never really happened;
- saying sorry;
- trying to forget;
- loving a person that you hate;
- excusing the person for their actions ('I'm sure they didn't really mean to do it').

What then is forgiveness? Forgiveness is the process by which you ruthlessly face the truth of the way in which you have been sinned against, express your emotions concerning the event, and then make a conscious choice to let go of your resentment and desire for revenge, handing the need for justice into God's own hands.

Facing the sin

The Holy Spirit is the spirit of truth, and it is only truth that sets us free. In order to forgive someone fully, we have to face the true nature of their sin against us, just as God knows the true nature and extent of our sin and then forgives us. If we excuse their actions and then forgive the illusion that we have created, we will not have truly forgiven the person in question.

Sarah did not want to have to face the truth that her parents had not loved her. She still clung desperately to the illusion that they were loving and caring people. Sadly, the evidence pointed in the opposite direction, but she had learned to see their physical abuse of her as loving behaviour because she believed she had deserved it. In order for Sarah to forgive her parents it was necessary to talk for a long time, gently helping her see that locking a child in a cupboard was not a loving form of discipline but was in fact sinful behaviour. Finally she felt prepared to begin letting go of false loyalty to her parents, and as she did so the real emotions in her heart, hidden away for all those years, began to rise to the surface. Instead of excusing their behaviour she began to see it as shocking and repulsive. Anger acts as a protective covering over emotional pain; as Sarah expressed her anger she began to feel the deep pain of the fear and loneliness in her own heart. She was now in a place to truly forgive her parents. To have forgiven them at an earlier stage would have been an illusion and would have done more damage than good. We must ask God for the Holy Spirit's help to see the truth, and for his courage to face it, however awful it may be.

'Place the person into God's hands'

God is a God of justice and no sin will go unpunished. 'When the time comes for me to punish, I will punish them for their sin' (Exodus 32:34). Every sin will be paid for, by Christ on the cross or by the person themselves having to bear the dreadful penalty of their sin before a holy God on Judgment Day.

Only God knows the state of a person's heart, and only God is able to be angry with sin without the anger turning into bitterness and a desire for personal revenge. That is why, in Romans 12:19, Paul teaches: 'Do not take revenge, my friends, but leave room for God's wrath, for it is written: "It is mine to avenge; I will repay," says the Lord.'

Because all sin will one day be dealt with, we can let the person in question go and place them into God's hands for him to deal with them as he sees fit. The Hebrew word *salach*, translated 'forgiveness', means 'to send off' or 'to let go'. Forgiveness such as this is not primarily a matter of the emotions but a matter of the will. We make a conscious choice to release the person from our own limited judgment, and place them into the hands of the Judge who is perfect in his justice and mercy. As we do this we consciously and deliberately, by an act of the will, give up the right to exact our revenge and make the person pay for their crime.

Forgiveness is God's strategy for releasing us from the damage that sinful people do to one another. All attempts to leave the past behind without releasing forgiveness are doomed to failure. Without forgiveness we will constantly live in reaction to the offending person and will remain emotionally attached to them by cords of bitterness and hatred. We will never be free from them until we cut the cord with the power of forgiveness. Forgiveness looses the offending person from our anger and looses us from their influence. As we forgive, we cease to remain the passive victim and rise up to become one who initiates and chooses life. Stuck in bitterness and resentment, we will for ever be looking for pity and revenge, and in doing so will miss those opportunities that God offers us to grow in maturity and wholeness.

Releasing resentment

I have only ever truly hated one person. The feeling of hatred was tangible. In those moments when I got in touch with it, it overwhelmed me with a strong desire to hurt the person involved. Anger and violence are never far apart. This hatred came to a head one day as I was sitting on a bus. I knew that God was wanting me to forgive, but I did not want to let go of the anger. I did not want to let the person off. All the hatred stored in my heart began to rise to the surface and I wondered how these powerful emotions could ever be taken away as they felt so deep and ingrained. After much struggling I chose to forgive him and to release him back to God. At the same time I chose to let go of all my resentment and bitterness. The effect was like bursting a balloon. All the twisted feelings flowed out of me and by the time I stepped off the bus, I could scarcely believe that my heart could be so free from the hatred that I had felt so acutely.

When we forgive we must choose to release the negative emotions back to the Lord. In so doing we appropriate the power of the cross and are enabled to begin receiving the light of the Lord into those areas that have been darkened by our sinful emotions. The blood of Jesus purifies our own hearts (1 John 1:9) and enables the long-held anger and pain to be cleansed and healed.

Not all forgiveness is completed at the first attempt. Forgiveness is like peeling an onion; you need to go down through the layers until there is nothing left, but each fresh layer will sting your eyes. My experience of the power of forgiveness on the bus was dramatic, but unusual. More often than not, I have had to forgive a person many times for wrongs done against me before all vestiges of the anger have gone. Each act of forgiveness carries with it emotional pain. True forgiveness is never easy. The process of forgiveness is not over until you are able to consider the person without rage or bitterness and can genuinely pray for their blessing.

John looked at me with pleading eyes and cried out in anguish, 'Can't I forget about the past and just move on? Can't I forgive without looking back?' Forgiveness would be so much easier if we could do it at a theoretical level, but forgiveness from the head is not the same as forgiveness from the heart. Jesus taught us to forgive from the heart (Matthew 18:35) and in order to do so we need to work towards forgiving in the midst of the emotions of pain and anger, shame and rage. It was from the cross and not the resurrection garden that Jesus cried out, 'Father, forgive them, for they know not what they do.'

It is when we are feeling most angry or most wounded that we should release the power of forgiveness. If we try to forgive without expressing our emotions from the heart, then the pain and anger will remain untouched. Anger that won't go away means that forgiveness has not been fully released, nor the underlying wound fully healed.

Forgiveness is a choice, it is a process and it involves the emotions. Here is a prayer that you might like to pray or adapt to help you forgive:

_____ *[insert person's name], I recognise today that the way you treated me was wrong and sinful. I name your sin before God. [Now name the sin done to you.]*

What you did to me made me feel _____.
[Acknowledge how it has made you feel.]

I choose today to let you go, and to place you into the hands of God in whom there is perfect justice. I will no

longer seek to make you pay for your actions or to gain my
revenge. I forgive you for what you have done to me.

Father God, I confess the anger and bitterness in my
heart and I choose to let it go. Please cleanse my heart and
heal my wounds with your love. Help me to one day pray
blessing upon this person I have just forgiven. Amen.

The healing love of God

Calvary always leads to resurrection. Dying to the false self
leads to the manifestation of the true self.

Our hearts are healed as we allow the unhealthy and twisted
emotions to be released into the body of Jesus, and receive the
life-giving power of his healing love as it pours into our innermost beings. Our love tanks are repaired and filled to overflowing. This is all part of God's perfect parenting of wounded
children. We are all grown-up children, and we are all
wounded to some degree from the effects of the fallen world.
God's love can reach down into our deepest point and there
replace the destructive emotions with a solid and unshakeable
sense of our safety, value and capability in him. In fact, it is as
though we become soaked through and through with his
unfailing, eternal and transforming love. In his love we find a
knowledge of our significance and identity, and we become
real.

In his letter to the Ephesians, Paul prays one of his glorious
apostolic prayers. It is a prayer for the emergence of the true
person, one who is filled to the measure of all the fullness of
God:

For this reason I kneel before the Father, from whom the whole
family in heaven and on earth derives its name. I pray that out of

his glorious riches he may strengthen you with power through his Spirit in your inner being, so that Christ may dwell in your hearts through faith. And I pray that you, being rooted and established in love, may have power together with all the saints, to grasp how wide and high and long and deep is the love of Christ and to know this love that surpasses knowledge – that you may be filled to the measure of all the fullness of God.

Now to him who is able to do immeasurably more than all we ask or imagine, according to his power that is at work within us . . . Amen. (Ephesians 3:20)

Paul is praying for the believers to receive the power of the Spirit in their inner beings, so that the real presence of Christ will dwell within them. But why should he pray this for men and women already regenerated by the Spirit? Because he knows that they need the reality of his love within their hearts. He prays that they will be *rooted* and *established* in love. The very foundations of our identity and existence become saturated with the love of God. This is the source of true maturity and personal wholeness. The wounded person who has walked the journey to wholeness is likely to know God at a more intimate level than the person who thinks that they have no need of healing. Having offered their hearts to him in faith and hope, they are able to receive his love into those same once-wounded hearts, and delight in the joy of intimacy that always accompanies true healing.

God is able to heal and restore us to a place which we once thought was beyond reach. He does this by his power at work within us. As his love is released into us, our thinking, our feeling and our choosing are infused with the reality of his love and we are able to become the people that we were created to be.

The healing of Ruth

Simon's wife Alison gave birth to little Ruth. She was their second child and they had been hoping for a little boy. They struggled to come to terms with a sense of profound disappointment at the arrival of their second girl. From day two of Ruth's life she had eczema on her body and appeared restless and anxious. She slept badly and her parents found her a difficult child compared to their first, who had been as good as gold. Both Simon and Alison tried desperately not to prefer the elder daughter, but they could not help but compare them. Just after Ruth's first birthday, her parents heard teaching on the healing power of God's love and the refilling of the love tanks. Kneeling beside Ruth's bed one evening they spoke to her in her sleep, asking her forgiveness for not meeting her emotional needs and affirming her in her own right as an infinitely valuable and precious person. Next they laid hands on Ruth and prayed that God would restore and refill her love tanks to full capacity, replacing the anxiety and filling the empty places.

Next morning they awoke to find a little girl with no trace of eczema. The anxiety at the root of her eczema had been healed by God's love as it filled her inner being. From that moment on, Ruth was much more secure in herself and less demanding; she also began to sleep better. Simon and Alison were thrilled.

One-year-olds cannot fake their own healing. God's love literally filled the heart and displaced the destructive emotions that were beginning to take root.

Made real by Jesus

The same healing process can take place in an adult who chooses to come to Christ and seek his presence in the midst of their pain. Even the most damaged and wounded person can know what it is to have a solid sense of identity in the love of God. Here is Andrea's testimony:

> Throughout my life I have felt that all the parts of me were scattered inside myself. Nothing about my inner world was substantial and solid. Bits of me were held together by anxiety and fear. I lived in constant turmoil, anxious about the future, full of self-doubt, fearfully looking backwards to try to identify mistakes I could avoid repeating in the present. It was as if I was curled in on myself. I felt misshaped and awkward, not fitting in, not really anyone. I knew Jesus loved me and was healing me, but it was never quite enough to know these things. I needed something else to make me well.
>
> Three days ago I was prayed for, and as a result my inner world has changed completely. It is as if Jesus literally walked into me and took up residence within, to replace all that anxiety, turmoil, doubt and fear. I feel alive. Jesus' presence within me is so powerful he has driven the darkness away. Somehow he has drawn all those scattered parts of me together so that I have become real and solid. Being a woman is no longer about my external appearance or copying other people who seemed to have what I didn't. It is something contained within me that Jesus has blessed and is calling out because he lives in me. Being able to take my eyes off myself is a genuine possibility and I have enjoyed being me these past few days. I want to live the rest of my life being me with him.

This deep healing was imparted to her after much pain and many tears and a constant seeking of Christ in her emotional turmoil. I believe it was her dedication to truth and pursuit of holiness that enabled Christ to enter her heart at such a deep place. The door to her heart had slowly been opening, and at the right moment he had entered. God is love. He is solid and real. We too become solid and real as we are infused with his loving presence.

How we feed on Christ's love in a way that heals and restores our hearts is the subject of the final three chapters of this book. In the context of this chapter it needs to be understood that it is God's love that fills our hearts and replaces the destructive emotions that we have had stored in them over the years. There is no emotion or attitude that is too strong or too deep for the love of God to deal with. No matter where we have come from or what we have done, the vision that God has for our lives is that each one of us should be filled to the measure of all the fullness of God. As our souls are flooded with the love of God, we will increasingly become the people that God made us to be and to know the wonder of his all-consuming love. In the presence of his love the real me is able to stand up.

Father God, I choose to align my will with yours. I am prepared to choose life in the midst of pain and temptation. Please show me my own heart. Give me the grace to forgive those who have failed me or sinned against me, and the grace to receive forgiveness for my own sinful responses. I invite you into the deep places of my inner being to establish my identity in your love. Replace all my destructive emotions with your solid, loving presence. Thank you, dear Lord. Amen.

EXERCISES

1. Spend a few moments in prayer and invite the Lord to show you the state of your will. Wait expectantly for a word, picture or intuitive knowing. In your journal write out or draw what he reveals to you. Choose now to align your will with God's will, and ask him to strengthen your will to choose life.

2. When you are in emotional pain or turmoil, what do you do to anaesthetise the feelings?

3. Invite the Lord to reveal to you anyone that you hold anger or bitterness against. Spend time forgiving from the heart.

4. With your eyes fixed on Christ, come to him to be loved. Invite him to pour his love into your heart.

Part 3

RENOUNCING FALSE COMFORTS

'Those who cling to worthless idols forfeit the grace
that could be theirs.' (Jonah 2:8)

8

Kicking the Habit

If we are to walk into maturity in Christ, and if we are to become all that God has made us to be, then the battle is on. Satan is our determined enemy and he will not let us grow and change without a fight: 'Be self-controlled and alert. Your enemy the devil prowls around like a roaring lion looking for someone to devour. Resist him, standing firm in the faith' (1 Peter 5:8–9).

The devil is your enemy and mine, and his purpose is to destroy God's ongoing work of salvation within you. As we seek to collaborate with all that Christ is doing within us we will undergo powerful demonic temptations to go back to our old ways. The false comforts that we used to run to will become intensely attractive to us once again. Where Satan has had an open door into our mind, emotions and will, he will battle to resist being shut out. We have to stand firm and resist the desires of our flesh to go back into captivity: 'It is for freedom that Christ has set us free. Stand firm, then, and do not let yourselves be burdened again by a yoke of slavery' (Galatians 5:1).

The new and real self will grow by the grace of God, but

only as we are prepared to put the old self to death. We must kick the habits that have been a part of our lives for so long, but in order to do so we must recognise their addictive power.

From choice to addiction

One day long ago, over the hot sands of a Middle Eastern country, a white skylark flew in joyous loops about the sky. As she swooped near the earth, she heard a merchant crying, 'Worms! Worms! Worms for feathers! Delicious worms!'

The skylark, realising how hungry she was, went to look at the merchant's wares and swapped one of her feathers for two of the beautiful and succulent worms. Day by day she returned to feed on the merchant's wares, exchanging her feathers for the tasty food. But one day as she tried to fly away she realised that she did not have enough feathers. Unable to fly she ran in terror across the desert to find a place to dig for worms. Finally, bloodied and bruised from her exertions, she carried her worms to the merchant. 'Oh merchant! Oh merchant! Please help me! Please take these worms from me and give me back my feathers!'

The merchant roared with laughter, took the worms and threw them into his jar. 'Oh, I'll take your worms all right, my friend. But feathers? What will you do with feathers? Glue them on with spit?' He cackled at his own joke. 'Besides, that's not my business – feathers for worms. Oh no . . .' he threw the skylark into a cage '. . . my business is WORMS FOR FEATHERS!' The merchant slammed the little cage door shut, smiled hungrily and vanished into thin air.[1]

The skylark's choices led to bondage and death. Slowly and imperceptibly she lost her freedom to her appetites, which had been skilfully manipulated by the evil merchant. Satan only has as much influence in our lives as we give him, but he seeks to exert control over us through manipulating the twisted and compulsive desires of our old nature. We all have sinful desires, but these desires will become habits, and our habits unchecked will become compulsions and our compulsions will become addictions. The difference between a habit and an addiction is a matter of degree.

Are you an addict?

What about you? Are you an addict? Do you have a craving that demands satisfaction? Do you have a habitual sin that you cannot seem to break free from? Addictions come in all shapes and sizes and none of us is very far from being addicted in some form or other. I have struggled with addiction, and maybe you do too.

The list of things that we can be addicted to is endless. Here are a few that are found in every church Sunday by Sunday: anger, approval, being right, being good, caffeine, chocolate, control, computers, diets, drugs, fantasy, fishing, fitness, films, golf, hobbies, image, lying, masturbation, money, perfection, power, relationships, romance, rules, religion, status, security, success, sex, stress, shopping, television, telephone, and work.

The heart of the matter

The primary issue at the heart of our habitual sins and addictive behaviour, whatever it may be, is not what we are addicted to but what the addiction does for us. What need is it meeting in me that drives me on to live in a way that is destructive and which dishonours Christ, who saved me? Addictions are present in our lives because they appear to bring comfort from emotional pain and respite from the fear of facing our own insecurity and inadequacy. They anaesthet-ise the pain inside.

If you have not faced your own potentially addictive desires and dealt with them in a creative and effective way, then you are almost certainly being influenced by them at an uncon-scious level. It has been said that only 20 per cent of our deci-sions are made at a rational and conscious level, while our unconscious mind determines 80 per cent of our decisions. The work of the Spirit of truth is to bring purity and holiness to all our motives – those that are conscious and those that are not. In order for this to happen, we must be willing to let him bring into the open anything that has been motivating us in unseen ways.

Signs of addiction

How can I know whether I am addicted or not? The follow-ing questions are helpful in revealing signs of addiction:

1. *Do I want more of it?*

I love salt on my food. The trouble is that the palate gets used to it, and so I need more salt to sustain the taste. The same is true of addictions. The body will need increasing amounts of the chemical or drug to reproduce the initial feelings. The heart also demands increasing amounts of the love, success or comfort to satisfy it. The more you have, the more you will want. Like a hungry dog, our sinful nature cries out to be satis-fied, but never is. The initial 'high' that the person, job, drink or success gives you will dull, only to be replaced by an even greater need for more of the same. I have been addicted to approval. After preaching I have often felt an intense and almost physical need for encouragement and approval that is only temporarily satisfied by someone's encouraging words. It was as though I had a sink hole in my heart through which the approval drained out, leaving me hungry for more. Our addictions demand to be fed, but they are never satisfied.

2. Do I feel anxious or stressed when denied it?

We have all seen images of drug addicts experiencing 'cold turkey', but when I was denied approval (after a lousy sermon!) I too had my own brand of withdrawal anxiety. I would feel worthless and inadequate and look for other ways to gain approval.

Coming off coffee or tea leaves us with a headache and feeling irritable and impatient. What happens when you cannot see your soulmate, your boy/girlfriend or your spouse? How do you feel when you have nothing to do and are alone with your own company? What is your reaction when the bank balance is low and there is nothing to spend on those little extras that you enjoy so much?

Once we begin to be denied access to our 'fix', the underlying needs that we try so hard to keep quiet or hidden come to the surface, leaving us anxious, lonely, fearful and desperate. No wonder we do not want to face the inner pain and brokenness. It hurts!

3. Do I justify my habits and behaviour?

Self-justification is the cornerstone on which addiction is built. We can find endless arguments to protect ourselves from admitting our own sin. The husband who finds meaning and worth through his work says, 'I am only doing it for the family [or the Lord], so that they can have everything that they need.' In saying this he attributes selfless motives to his self-centred pursuit of value and significance.

Another form of self-justification is to compare our own addiction with those of people we think are more addicted than ourselves.

'At least I am not addicted to sex,' says the workaholic.

'At least I am not a drug addict,' thinks the control freak.

'At least I am not a comfort eater,' says the shopaholic.

We have innumerable ways of justifying our own sin while condemning that which we see in others. It is crucial for the person driven by compulsive desires to deny that they exist. To stop the self-justification is to admit that we have failed and need help, but it is the last thing our pride wants to do. We do not want to face the pain and we do not want any help!

As the saying goes, 'Touch an addiction – get a reaction'.[2] If you are sensitive and touchy when certain habits or attitudes are pointed out to you, take note – you may well be protecting yourself from the truth.

4. Do I believe that I can overcome the problem in my own strength?

'I can stop whenever I want to!' is the addict's classic statement, but this is all part of the elaborate facade that is used to protect ourselves from the need to change. And it is invariably accompanied by the unspoken thought: 'but I don't want to yet!'

The quickest way to discover whether you have an addiction is to stop doing it. Not for one day or one week, but for several months. That way you will find out the degree of hold that it has on you.

We like to believe that we are strong and in control, lest we have to face our own impotence and weakness and admit that we are not the person we are so busy convincing others to believe in.

5. Are my thoughts increasingly focused on it?

Compulsive eaters spend a large proportion of the waking day thinking about what they will eat next. Women addicted to the great god 'slim' find that their thinking is focused on calories and fitness programmes. The man addicted to proving his sexual prowess constantly schemes how he will bed the next girl.

What do you think about most through the day? In times of quiet when nothing is being demanded of you, what absorbs your imagination and your desires? Whatever it is will reveal that which you are serving, and to which you are addicted.

We are all potential addicts

Every single one of us has the capacity to become addicted in one form or another. We all have unmet emotional needs that are rooted in our childhoods and manifested in our lives as adults. We are all looking for comfort, security, fulfilment and achievement. These are God-given needs at the core of our humanity. The issue is not whether we have these needs but what we do to meet them. If we do not first press into Christ to allow him to meet all our needs, then we will turn away from the Creator and seek to find what we need from the creation. In this way we are led into idolatry.

> Although they claimed to be wise, they became fools and exchanged the glory of the immortal God for images made to look like mortal man and birds and animals and reptiles . . . They exchanged the truth of God for a lie, and worshipped and served created things rather than the creator – who is for ever praised. Amen. (Romans 12:22–5)

The more wise our culture considers itself to be, the more foolish it in fact becomes. Puffed up in its own eyes, society sees little need for a God when it believes that it can solve its own problems. We Christians appear to be squeezed into its mould, as we too look to materialism to meet our physical and emotional needs. The church is full of men and women who believe in God's existence, understand the concept of the cross and the resurrection, but day by day find themselves bowing down to the gods of this age. Not knowing how to feed on Christ in a way that satisfies the cry of their hearts, they fall for the lie of the devil and seek fulfilment in the creation.

In Colossians 3:4, Paul declares that 'Christ is your life'. It is the indwelling presence of Christ that transforms us. As we have seen, we become new creations, born of the Spirit with unrestricted access to the source and giver of life. When we succumb to addictive behaviour, then we deny our new identities and try to meet our physical and emotional needs apart from him. Apart from him we wither and die.

When we tolerate the presence of habits, addictions and false comforts in our lives we are engaging in idol worship, and we fail to take hold of the grace that has already been provided for us through the presence of Christ within us: 'Those who cling to worthless idols forfeit the grace that could be theirs' (Jonah 2:8). This is a dangerous position to be in. To allow sinful behaviour to remain a part of our lives, however innocuous it may be, is to open the door to demonic infestation and satanic deception.

> The object of the sinful compulsion slowly erodes and replaces all other desires, eventually even displacing God himself, the one who should be the object of our deepest yearning. In this way we literally worship and fall into the grip of part of the creation instead of the creator.[3]

Addictions grow in power and control. To tolerate any addiction is to be in danger of giving the sinful nature (and the demons that can hide in the sinful nature) control over areas of our lives. This is something that we must never do. We are called to be perfect as our Father in heaven is perfect. I once heard someone say that a little sin is good for you. Such a view, so influenced by the prevailing culture, is foolish and totally misunderstands the seductive, and truly destructive, nature of sin.

The addictive cycle

Addiction does not just happen; it follows a well researched and documented cycle. The one set out below has been used by counsellors dealing with alcohol and drug addiction, but as I hope you will see it is relevant to all forms of addiction, habitual sins and compulsive behaviour.

Let's look in more detail at how the addictive cycle actually works.

1. *Love hunger*

We have already seen that when our emotional needs for security, value and significance are not met, we are left with

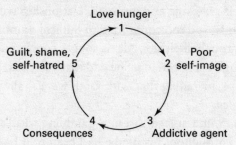

Figure 9 – The addictive cycle

love tanks that are inadequately filled. Because none of us has had perfect parents we are all hungry for love.

Alexis grew up in a very busy household. Her father was a clergyman and there were always people coming and going. Not only was her dad a workaholic and emotionally distant, but her mother experienced depression and emotional break-down. Alexis's needs were always second to 'God's work'. Although she had two brothers, their relationship was highly competitive, each seeking to win those few scraps of love that were on offer. Alexis grew up to be highly sociable but devoid of satisfying and intimate relationships. Whenever her pain surfaced she would run to her friends and drown the hurt with her social life.

2. Poor self-image and low self-esteem

When our foundational needs are not met we have a poor self-image and low self-esteem. Alexis felt inadequate, insecure and insignificant. She found it hard to believe anyone would want to spend time with her, and did not dare reveal her inner self to anyone lest she should be rejected.

3. Addictive agent

For Alexis the addictive agent was people. Too fearful to pursue a self-revealing and intimate relationship with male or female friends, and too committed to biblical morality to seek intimacy through illicit sex, Alexis sought comfort and signifi-cance through her social life. She had many friends, but all her relationships, including that with God, were shallow and left her unfulfilled.

Nicholas found solace through gambling, drink and por-nography. Throughout his life he had been told he was inad-equate and that he would never amount to much. When he did succeed, the affirmation and sense of achievement never materialised. Nicholas had found some sense of self-worth through his music and had become a worship leader in a lively local church. He kept his addiction secret, and continued to play the part of a happy and fulfilled Christian.

Addictive agents are not necessarily inherently addictive (like alcohol or tobacco) but become addictive when they give us the pleasure or sense of well-being that we are seeking. The addictive agent is used as a false comfort because we do not trust Christ to meet our needs through his love and power.

4. Consequences

Every addiction has consequences that impact our lives and the lives of those around us. The comfort eater finds him/herself becoming overweight or even obese. The gambler learns to lie to his wife as money to pay the bills disappears. The control addict ends up manipulating his friends or his family and wonders why his relationships seem so shallow.

No sin is individualistic in the sense that it harms no one but the perpetrator. All sin, including habits and addictions, will affect both God and those with whom we have relationships.

5. Guilt, shame, self-hatred

Nicholas's addiction to gambling, drink and pornography leaves him feeling guilty and ashamed. In his more perceptive moments he recognises that he hates himself for being too weak to change and too cowardly to admit his problem to his church leaders. Alexis feels guilty when she manipulates her friends to meet her need for company and attention. Because the addict's love tanks are so low and self-esteem so fragile, guilt, shame and self-hatred are never far away and surface again when the addiction fails to meet the deep needs of the heart. All addicts will experience times of great guilt, shame and self-hatred. When the anaesthetic wears off, they are left to face their own behaviour and the inevitable consequences. These times of painful self-awareness can become opportunities for change. It is painful when the Holy Spirit convicts us of our sin, and it is meant to be. He convicts us to get our attention and to wake us up to our real and present danger.

'Godly sorrow brings repentance that leads to salvation and leaves no regrets, but worldly sorrow brings death' (2 Corinthians 7:10). Godly sorrow leads us back to the cross where we have to face our sickness of soul and desperate need of cleansing. This brings life. Worldly sorrow is where we are merely saddened that something wrong has taken place, but excuses us from personal responsibility. Modern secular psychologists run from the term 'sin', seeing it as judgmental and prejudiced, and yet it is only as we name and confess our sin that we can leave it at the cross. Jesus Christ did not die for our weaknesses or our little foibles, he died for our *sins*! Guilt and remorse are God's gift to mankind to warn us of our wrongdoing. As Mark Twain said, 'Man is the only animal that blushes – and needs to!'

6. *Love hunger*

The addiction cannot meet the needs of our hearts and we are left as empty as we were before. Many times we are left even more empty and even more anxious and so we begin the cycle again. The addiction that seemed to provide the answer to our inner pain has now become the cause. The addictive cycle grips our lives even more tightly and pulls us downward in a destructive spiral.

The snowball effect

No habitual sin or addiction will stay within safe boundaries. Their very nature is to grow and become all-consuming.

> Picture a child at the crest of a hill, fashioning a large, icy snowball. He checks the fall line, assures himself no rocks or trees stand in the way, and shoves the snowball over the side. It's a long hill. Clunky and uncertain at first, the snowball slowly picks up weight, speed, momentum. Halfway down it has already burgeoned into a Godzilla of a monster, mindless and unstoppable. By the time it reaches the bottom and rolls relentlessly across the creek gully, it has become the Snowball of Death. The addiction cycle is that snowball.[4]

Because addictions invariably come in clusters, if we allow one to take any sort of grip in our lives it makes us vulnerable to others. The large snowball picks up other snowballs on the way down the hill, increasing its destructive capability. It's easy to see the threat to life that heroin or crack presents, but what about the more subtle addictions, such as approval or success? I may have a perfectly respectable life, be the stalwart of my church and see God using me in wonderful ways, but if I am operating out of subtle and hidden strongholds then I am still addicted and open to greater temptations. If I do not deal with my addictions now, whatever their power or influence on my life at the moment, then I am deluding myself and am in more bondage than I care to admit.

Denial

Just as cement holds a house together, so denial keeps the addictive cycle intact. Thoughts, feelings and motives are denied access to our consciousness in order to prevent us from having to confront their reality. We simply refuse to accept the reality of their presence and so protect ourselves from needing to change. We go on living in just the same way. Denial is not so much a conscious act of self-deception as an unconscious defence mechanism that protects us from pain. Denial is the way in which we try to block out the source of our unease and so create 'reality' to suit ourselves.

Paul was known by his friends at school as the kid with the 'Kellogg's family'. Paul and his family gave the appearance of perfection, but behind the facade was a violent father and a traumatic family life. They never discussed the root issues of their problems, and in order to be loyal to the family unit they learned to present an acceptable front. Because they never faced their own sickness, they could not let anyone else see it either. Paul learned the art of denial within his family and it continued into his adult life. A family that can address its own problems and face them honestly together, where the parents and children ask for forgiveness and freely give it, teaches the child to be real with their emotions and to face that which is painful. Very few families have parents as secure and healthy as this and so the art of denial is passed down through the generations. Denial breeds denial.

Once we have learned the art of denial it operates unseen and enables us to blank out our problems. When in denial we have no idea that we are doing it. The essence of deception is that we do not know we are in it when we are in it! The following phrases are indications of our denial:

- It's not as bad as you think.
- It's not an addiction, I am just going through a hard time.
- I will change, just you wait and see. It's just the way I am.

- I don't need any help. I can do it on my own.
- It's not my problem; it's yours.

The Spirit of truth

The first step out of an addiction or habitual sin is to admit its presence. The work of the Holy Spirit is to lead us into all truth. If we are truly prepared to pursue the journey to maturity in Christ then we must first come to him and invite him to reveal to us our hidden habits and addictions and their root causes.

But how will he show us what they are? The conscience acts as the alarm system of the soul. God will prick our conscience if we dare let him, giving us a growing sense of unease over a particular habit or attitude. However, it does not have to be as subjective as that. People in denial are often very much at ease with their denial; it is an old friend that they would not want to be without. Their consciences may have become seared (1 Timothy 4:12) and impervious to the prompting of the Spirit. In addition to our consciences, God has given us friends: brothers and sisters in Christ to whom we must learn to be accountable and who have the loving right to speak truth into our lives if we will give them permission. It is important, even crucial, that we invite a small number of trusted friends to have the freedom to speak into our lives if they see anything in us that is not Christlike. The perception of others is one of the greatest safeguards against self-deception. We must test their words, but first we must listen with humble and open hearts.

God used my wife to get through to me. As I listened to her the Spirit showed me the true state of my heart, and in this way I began to come out of my own denial. God used Nathan to speak into King David's life after his affair with Bathsheba and his subsequent murder of her husband, Uriah the Hittite. David was in denial over his actions and God used an old prophet to wake him up to the horror of his deeds.

Pray for Nathans in your life, and having prayed for them be prepared to listen to those whom God sends you. They will surely come if you are committed to walking in freedom and to ridding your life of any addictions that would bind you.

Step two is to take action to control the use of the addictive agent in your life. This is repentance. Stop running to your friends whenever you are lonely – go to Christ in prayer. Stop controlling people and determine to let God have control of the relationships. Give up the caffeine shot and drink something else instead. If you are coming off chemical dependency, ensure that you seek the advice of a doctor.

Step three is to begin to work through the unresolved emotions in your life, which takes us back into Part 2 of this book. You may want to work through it again.

Step four is to build in good habits that will guard you from falling back into the old patterns, and which will enable you to feed on the life of Christ. That is the aim of Part 4 of this book.

The call to freedom

Jesus Christ came to set captives free, to release the oppressed and to preach the good news to the poor. The goal of the gospel and the work of the Spirit is to create men and women of God who walk in true freedom. Free from the manipulation of the society, free from the power of the sinful nature, they are empowered by the indwelling Christ to live lives of truth, authority and love. Tolerating addictions, of whatever sort, is to give away the birthright of freedom and to come again under bondage to sin. To do this is unthinkable to Paul: ' "Everything is permissible for me" – but not everything is beneficial. "Everything is permissible for me" – *but I will not be mastered by anything*' (1 Corinthians 6:12, italics mine).

It is foolish, idiotic – but we all do it! Thank God that we are already forgiven and holy in our new natures. Despite our weakness and deliberate rebellion, there is always the second, third, fourth . . . and fiftieth chance!

Father God, I thank you that you came to set me free from bondage to any form of addiction. I ask you to reveal to me through your Spirit and the discernment of my friends if there is any hidden addiction at work in my life. Please break through any denial that I might be in, and help me to face the pain and chaos within my own heart. I choose life in all its fullness and I choose to put to death all addictive behaviour of which I am already aware or of which I may become aware in the future. Thank you. Amen.

EXERCISES

1. Are you able to identify any addictions at work within members of your family? Describe what they are/were and what their impact on you has been.

2. Apply the addictive cycle to your own life and fill in your own personal details in each section. Seek to be as candid as possible with yourself. On a continuum of 0–10 mark the point where you would place your habit/addiction:

    HABIT 0 1 2 3 4 5 6 7 8 9 10 ADDICTION

3. How did your family cope with problems? In what ways did you learn the art of denial from your family?

4. Go back to the section on denial. Consider the different phrases that are used to reinforce denial: are you aware of using any of these yourself? What form does denial take in your life? What is it that you are seeking to protect yourself from facing?

5. What actions do you need to take to accept personal responsibility for breaking your own addiction?

9

Easing the Pain

Over the past twenty years we have seen a marked increase in the breakdown of the fabric of our society. Spiralling divorce rates, increased levels of sexual immorality, a growing acceptance of short-term relationships as an alternative to marriage, huge numbers of abortions and the abandonment of biblical values have created an enormous pool of pain and trauma in people's lives. This is fertile ground for the growth of dependent and addictive behaviour on an unprecedented scale. In this chapter we will look at three forms of dependency that are prevalent within our culture and which are likely to exert an influence on every single one of us.

Emotional dependency

Geoff and Sally had been leading a home group in their local church for a number of years. When they decided it was time for the group to come to an end, all the members agreed that it was the right decision, even though they would miss the support that it had provided. All of them, that is, except Jim. Jim felt abandoned and accused Geoff and Sally of not caring. He made threats and shed tears, tried to make them feel guilty for giving up, and argued persistently to make them change their minds. It became increasingly apparent that his security had been in the loving care of his leaders rather than in Christ himself. Now that the group was disbanding, Jim's desperate need for their attention and support had been revealed. He was emotionally dependent on his leaders to such an extent that it was jeopardising his relationship with Christ.

When Tim and Anna met it was love at first sight. They were both committed to Christ and determined to centre their relationship on him. All went well for the first few months, but slowly Tim noticed a change in Anna. She became increasingly clingy and in need of his affirmation. She looked to him to make all their decisions and she would hold his hand and seek to cuddle him at every possible opportunity. Tim felt suffocated and began to withdraw emotionally, causing Anna to cling to him even more tightly. Whenever she thought he was not being attentive, Anna would accuse Tim of not really loving her. He would have to promise once again that he would never leave her, and then she would go out and buy him a present to remind him of their undying love. Realising that she was sucking him dry emotionally, he wanted to end the relationship but was fearful of the effect it would have on her.

Replacing the pain with a person

Emotional dependency takes place when we look to a person to fill the emptiness that we feel inside. It is as though we have an imaginary umbilical cord attached to our innermost being and we plug it into a person who gives us the love and attention we have always longed for. Once this umbilical cord is fixed, we cry out in endless unspoken ways: 'FEED ME! MEET MY NEEDS! YOU ARE THE ONLY ONE!'

Jim was feeding off his healthy leaders, and Anna was feeding off Tim's strength and attention. We all have appropriate emotional needs that will be met by healthy relationships, but no one person can meet all our needs. Emotionally dependent people feed off other people to compensate for their own sense of emptiness. Not having a solid sense of their own being and identity, the emotionally dependent man or woman seeks to find themselves through the attention of another. The degree to which we look first to people and not to God to meet our needs will reveal the extent of our emotional dependence.

Emotional dependence can be found in same-sex and cross-sex friendships, in home groups, between church members and church leaders, husbands and wives, counsellors and counsellees. Men and women, old and young, rich and poor, all can be emotionally dependent. Whenever a person with low or empty love tanks looks to another person to fill up what is lacking in themselves, there is emotional dependence. In her book *Emotional Dependency* Lori Rentzel identifies eleven signs that distinguish between normal relational interdependence and unhealthy dependency. Emotional dependency is likely to be operating when one or both persons in a relationship:

- experiences frequent jealousy, possessiveness and a desire for exclusivism, viewing other people as a threat to the relationship;
- prefers to spend time alone with the other, and becomes frustrated when this doesn't happen;
- becomes irrationally angry or depressed when the other withdraws slightly;

- loses interest in other friendships;
- experiences romantic or sexual feelings that lead to fantasy about this person;
- becomes preoccupied with the other person's appearance, personality, problems and interests;
- is unwilling to make short- or long-term plans that do not include the other person;
- is unable to see the other's faults realistically;
- displays physical affection beyond what is appropriate for a friendship;
- refers frequently to the other in conversation; feels free to 'speak for' the other;
- exhibits an intimacy and familiarity with this friend that causes others to feel uncomfortable or embarrassed in their presence.[1]

God has designed us to need healthy, open and intimate relationships with one another. Healthy friendships are generous, inclusive and freeing. In a healthy relationship I am happy to include others and extend the blessing of the friendship to them. I am also enabled to be myself. In an unhealthy friendship that shows signs of dependency it will be exclusive, protective, suffocating, anxious and defensive.

At the heart of authentic love is the desire to see the other person grow and develop to become all that God wants them to be. This must mean that we are prepared to release them if they should choose to end the relationship. Authentic love is highly vulnerable. But this enabling and freeing love is anathema to the emotionally dependent person. They 'need too much' to allow the possibility that the other person might choose to walk away.

Dependent people are interested in their own nourishment, but no more; they desire filling, they desire to be happy; they don't desire to grow nor are they willing to tolerate the unhappiness, the loneliness and the suffering involved in growth. Neither do dependent people care about the spiritual growth of the other, the object of their dependency. They care only that the other is there to satisfy them.[2]

Manipulation

Because the fear of losing the friendship is so real, manipulation is the vital tool that the dependent person will use to keep the other person in the relationship. Manipulation is using your influence or power to control or determine another's behaviour in subtle or hidden ways. An action or comment that appears innocent may in fact be manipulative; *the key is the intention*. If your aim is to get the person to do something that you want, but without you saying it openly, then you are being manipulative. The trouble is that very often people are so used to being manipulative, perhaps from childhood, that they do not consciously see their behaviour as wrong.

Here are some examples of manipulation:

- giving financial gifts in such a way as to leave the recipient indebted to you;
- giving presents that reinforce the uniqueness of the relationship;
- using flattery and approval, such as 'You're the only one who really loves me' or 'I don't know what I would do without you';
- using tears or cold silences to make the other feel bad or guilty at having upset you;

- undermining the other person's relationships that make you feel threatened;
- making threats to end the relationship, to commit suicide, to sabotage agreed plans.

These are by no means the only ways to manipulate but they are some of the most common. It is not wrong to cry when hurt or to give special little gifts, but if the intention is to control the person or bind them to you, then it is manipulation.

As we saw in Chapter 8, we are all potential addicts, and emotional dependence is all too common in Christian circles, where it masquerades as supportive and intimate relationships but is in fact another form of idolatry. We look to the creature to meet our needs before turning to the Creator. We are particularly susceptible to slipping into dependent relationships at times of anxiety, stress or loneliness, for instance when a previous relationship has ended or there has been the death of a close relative or friend. Times of change when we move house or job, or periods when the pressure at work or at home is intense and exhausting, leave us vulnerable to starting emotionally dependent relationships.

A relationship that is emotionally dependent will ultimately be dissatisfying. Though it may begin with the promise of real fulfilment, it will become increasingly manipulative, suffocating and destructive. The frustration and disappointment that accompanies emotionally dependent relationships leaves us hungry and thirsty for something deeper and more substantial. If we are prepared to face our behaviour and the underlying needs that we are attempting to meet in a person, then we can begin to seek God in order to know his love that will satisfy our deepest needs and create in us a sense of our own completeness in him. When this takes place we no longer need another person to make us feel complete. We know we are complete in Christ.

Co-dependency

Co-dependency is another form of relationship addiction. When a person who is insecure in their own personal identity seeks to find their sense of self by meeting another person's needs and solving their problems, they have become co-dependent.

Michelle grew up with an alcoholic father who would often come home from work drunk, abusive and violent. Her mother was a submissive person with strong morals. She saw it as her role in life to look after this man and to try to restore him to good health and a sober life. She would ring the office to explain that he was ill when in fact he was too drunk to get out of bed; she would make sure the children were well dressed and presentable even when there was not enough money to cover the food bills. Often her mother would be unable to cope, so Michelle learned to run the home, cook the food and keep everyone happy. The times when she knew most approval and love were when she was shouldering the responsibility for the rest of the family.

As a grown woman, she determined never to marry an alcoholic. She would find herself a strong and dependable man. When she met Keith, she quickly fell in love with him. He was strong and good-looking, successful at his career and very attentive to her needs. He might work a bit too hard and drink a little too much, but she knew that she could help him straighten those things out. She saw his vulnerable side and knew that she would be good for him. After they were married, she found that the drinking grew worse and he worked even longer hours. She covered up for his drunken binges, cleared up the bottles, loved and encouraged him and generally kept the peace. On the odd occasion that he hit her she would explain it away to her friends, and anyway she thought that she had deserved it for upsetting him.

Michelle is a classic example of a co-dependent. Growing up in a damaged and dysfunctional home, her own love needs unmet, she learned that her role was to look after others. By denying her own valid needs, she found her worth in supporting those around her. If there was a need, she felt impelled to meet it whatever the cost to herself; not to have done so would have felt unloving, immoral and unbearably selfish. Like all co-dependents, she lived in a fantasy world in which she constantly looked forward to the day when she would be able to sort things out for everyone else. When she met Keith, he appeared to be all she wanted in a man. Her 'magical' thinking enabled her to focus on his good points and ignore his rather obvious weaknesses. While she did not like his drinking and overcommitment to work she was convinced she could change him. At a more unconscious level she felt at home with him. She knew what it was like to look after men with problems, and Keith enabled her to dance again the steps that she had learned in her family. When all was said and done, Michelle needed Keith for her own self-worth.

If she dared look closely Michelle would see that her dependence is every bit as powerful as his. He needs his alcohol and work, and she needs him to stay needing his alcohol and his work. Unwittingly she is enabling Keith to stay in his addiction, while giving herself and everyone else the impression that she is doing everything in her power to redeem him.

Learned behaviour

Co-dependency is learned behaviour, and can develop in any family that teaches a child to deny his own needs and find acceptance and love through looking after others. According to *The California Lawyer* (November 1989) the family most likely to produce co-dependents has these characteristics:

- a parent exercising inflexible control, or whose needs dominate the family;
- secrecy – problems and emotions are not talked about;
- denial – problems and emotions do not exist;
- concern with appearances – look good at all costs;
- isolation – emotional and sometimes physical isolation, from each other and outsiders.

Members of these families live by three commandments: thou shalt not talk (about problems or emotions); thou shalt not trust; thou shalt not feel.[3]

Obviously these different characteristics are not just found in the families of alcoholics; in fact almost all families are influenced by them to one degree or another. The potential for producing co-dependent behaviour relates to both the degree to which these five characteristics are present and the personality of the child. Strongly religious families can all too easily produce co-dependents if laws and rules are prioritised above the emotional needs of the children.

Co-dependent traits

The following are some traits that are common to co-dependents:

1. *A co-dependent is a driven person*   Their behaviour is driven by compulsive desires: 'I must be helpful', 'I need to be involved', 'I couldn't possibly say "no"'. Driven by compulsion, they feel they have little choice over their own decisions.

2. *The co-dependent is bound and tormented by the way things were done in their own family*   Unable to shake themselves free from the past they keep making the same mistakes they saw their parents make.

3. *A co-dependent is certain their happiness depends on others*   Having no intrinsic sense of self-worth, they rely on others to give them pleasure, happiness or freedom. A co-dependent is bound by the moods and decisions of others.

4. *Co-dependents feel inordinately responsible for others*   Having learned from a young age to be responsible for others, they quickly take on false responsibility in the name of self-sacrifice or true love. A key question they need to ask is: 'Whose problem is it?' Only once they have separated their identity from the person in need will they be in a position to respond appropriately.

5.   *The co-dependent's significant relationships are characterised by swings from dependence to independence*   Needing another's problem to give them meaning, they are highly dependent; but suffocated by their own involvement they break away to breathe again. Very soon their compulsive need to be needed pulls them back into the relationship.

As you read these traits, can you see anything of yourself in them? Co-dependency can present itself in more subtle ways than in the case of Michelle. What about the woman with the 'gift of helps' who is constantly helping out at the church but whose family or friends go unattended? Think for a moment of the husband who is continually helping needy people while his wife tears her hair out trying to look after the kids. She never complains for fear of stopping him doing 'the Lord's work'. His co-dependency focuses on the needs of others, and he may well be commended by his church for his 'sacrificial giving'.

In the caring professions there are many co-dependent men and women who are driven by their need to rescue others. Because of their lack of emotional stability they are unable to develop appropriate boundaries around their choices, and their priorities become distorted. Needing to be needed, they rush headlong into the needs of the world, only to burn out all too quickly. The caring professions have extremely high rates of breakdown and divorce, because the co-dependent is unable to care appropriately for their own health or the health of their spouse and family.

The example of Jesus

Because the Bible calls the Christian to self-sacrifice, co-dependency can all too easily pass off as true Christian service. One instance in Jesus' life reveals how far he was from being co-dependent, and gives us a model that distinguishes between true service and co-dependency:

> That evening . . . the whole town gathered at the door, and Jesus healed many who had various diseases. He also drove out many demons . . . Very early in the morning, while it was still dark, Jesus got up, left the house and went off to a solitary place where he

prayed. Simon and his companions went to look for him, and when they found him, they exclaimed, 'Everyone is looking for you!' Jesus replied, 'Let us go somewhere else – to the nearby villages – so that I can preach there also. That is why I have come.' So he travelled throughout Galilee, preaching in their synagogues and driving out demons. (Mark 1:32–7)

The people were thrilled, and so were the disciples! Jesus had the power to meet their needs in a way that no one had ever done before. But when the disciples, flushed with the triumph of the previous day, find him next morning, Jesus refuses to go back to the village. He chose not to meet the valid needs of those who were still crying out for his attention. Jesus was not co-dependent! He was not driven by a compulsive need to help others. Jesus was motivated by love, but love is freely given as a choice, it is never a compulsion. Jesus was able to say no to their need because he knew who he was and he knew why he had come. The key to this self-knowledge is his life of prayer. To the villagers and to the disciples his actions could have been seen as unloving and selfish. 'Doesn't he care?' they might have said. 'If he really loved me he would come and help!' Jesus was called to obey the Father; he was not driven to meet people's needs. He knew when to say yes and when to say no, because his ability to hear the Father's voice was not drowned out by his own need to be needed.

As we learn to find our own identity in Christ, to break away from our need to be needed and allow the Spirit to satisfy our deep hunger for significance, then we will be free to truly love those whom God has anointed us to serve. Freed from our inner compulsions, we will no longer burn ourselves out for God. We are free to say yes or to say no, to help or to refuse, to serve or to withdraw. Enabled by the Holy Spirit to give generously of our time and energy, we are also able to resist the pressure to do what others would want. Our relationships and our service will then be marked by the twin virtues of grace and truth.

Work dependence

Recently I spoke to a friend on the phone and asked him how he was doing. 'Fine,' he replied. 'I am very busy at the moment, work is going really well and I can see God using me in lots of ways.' I put the phone down, disturbed in my spirit but not quite sure why. I thought it over for a while and then it clicked: every time I asked him how he was he always replied in a way that was related to how hard he was working and how much he saw God using him. His success at work appeared to determine his emotional and spiritual state. It is not wrong to work hard, and it is wonderful to see God work through your life, but this should never be the barometer by which we evaluate ourselves. When my friend was not very busy he felt that people did not appreciate him and that God did not love him as much. In his head he knew that this was not true, but in his heart he knew little of what it meant to be loved irrespective of his performance.

The call to work

In the creation narrative in Genesis, we see that work is God-given. God himself is a worker who creates for six days and rests on the seventh: 'By the seventh day God had finished the *work* he had been doing; so on the seventh day he rested from all his *work*' (Genesis 2:2, italics mine).

God is a worker who expresses his will and creativity through his work. Man made in his image is also a worker: 'God blessed them and said to them, "Be fruitful and increase in number; fill the earth and subdue it. Rule over the fish of the sea and the birds of the air and over every living creature that moves on the ground" ' (Genesis 1:28).

Adam and Eve were commissioned to work, to bring the earth under their dominion and to rule over it. Work was to be an expression of their loving care of God's creation. The danger that we face in a fallen world is that we allow the pressure of our society's adoration of success and performance to draw us away from our first calling to live in intimate relationship with God and with one another. The drive to succeed is a flight from authentic relationships. We replace intimacy with performance. When we focus on our work and activity to restore to us the worth, value and significance that is only possible through relationship with God, then work will become idolatrous in our lives. Our call to work is to be an expression of our identity in Christ, and when this identity is solid then both our work and our relationships will find their proper balance within our lives.

The pressure to conform

If we do not run into relationships to find meaning, acceptance and value we are very likely to pursue them through activity and work. To succeed at work or in our chosen calling will earn the approval and respect of our peers, thereby offering to give us the identity that we are so desperately seeking. We live in a culture that idolises work and success and therefore exerts real pressure on each person to conform. Sociologist Tony Walter writes: 'We have arrived at a world in which work is idolised in the sense that economic performance is seen as an important measure of the worth of the individual and as the measure of the worth of a society.'[4]

Not only is there great pressure to value our intrinsic

worth according to our earning capacity, but for those who have renounced the pursuit of money there is still the pressure to value themselves according to the effectiveness of their work. I am talking about the housewife who values herself according to her ability to keep the home and the kids in perfect shape, or the charity worker who needs his boss's affirmation and approval and so lives for his job. Work dependence takes many different forms; it is not limited to the driven businessman. We often stereotype addictions in such a way that we can remain unchallenged in our own behaviour. It is easier to believe that it is someone else's problem and not our own!

Let us look at the five signs of dependence in relation to work.

1. Do I want more of it? A solid sense of identity cannot be found through activity, work or success. It is an illusion. The need to take on new projects, solve new problems, attain new heights of achievement, push for that better job, will only increase as the promise of personal peace and fulfilment goes unmet. We will need more power, more influence, more recognition to keep our underlying sense of meaninglessness at bay.

2. Do I get a stress reaction when denied it? How do you react when things go badly in your work? How do you react if you fail, if your boss or your peers do not recognise your efforts, or if you get passed over in the new round of promotions? We all have a need for recognition, affirmation and encouragement, but how we react when they are denied will often reveal a stronger craving than we are aware of when things are going well.

When we are denied the activity of work itself or the feelings that our work gives us, then we must take careful note of the stress reaction that follows. Some are left with a profound sense of failure and insignificance. It is as if they have no real meaning apart from their work and they are left to face their own sense of non-being. I have often felt unwanted and lonely when my day has not been full, as though my very identity has needed activity to determine its validity. Feeling insignificant, we quickly rush to find new challenges and activities to restore to us our sense of importance. If work is withdrawn we may feel incompetent. God intended that work should be the expression of our ability, and not the proof of it. If we do not know within ourselves that God has made us good, then we will seek to prove it through our achievements.

For others work makes them feel safe. To work means to earn a salary that will bring security and peace of mind. Obviously paid work is important to provide for yourself and your family, but the degree to which you strive to gain security through your work is likely to reveal more about your fears than about your trust in Christ. I recently spent time with a man who had known significant poverty in his early life, the memory of which had sent him on a search for financial security. Though he knew the Scriptures, his underlying fear of poverty was motivating him to work compulsively and to lose sight of his life's priorities. If we seek security through work, it will have a hold over us that will compromise our walk with Christ.

It is all too easy for us as Christians to interpret our driven need for achievement, power and recognition as being 'ambitious for God'. We cover our compulsions with a superficial spiritual veneer. At boarding school the physical and verbal bullying that I suffered left me feeling insignificant and inadequate. I believed that my worth and sense of competence would come through success. Fortunately I was good at golf and became the school's top player. Because I had tasted some success, I did not give up hope and drift into apathy. Instead I worked extremely hard and succeeded academically. Three months after leaving school I was converted and began to walk with Christ, but my underlying need for success was not destroyed. I became ambitious for God, both at work and at church! I had no idea I was doing it at the time, but my need for recognition and my longing to feel important drove me on. It wasn't until my wife began to complain of my inability to be still, of my restless need to achieve, that I began to realise that my 'Christian' ambition was simply a veneer on my need for a sense of my own significance. The motive for so much of what I did in the name of God was in fact deeply self-centred.

3. *Do I justify my habits and behaviour?* In order to protect ourselves from facing our own sin, we justify our behaviour in a way that makes it seem acceptable. In reality we are lying to ourselves.

'I work so hard in order to provide for my family.' But what if your wife and family would prefer to see you for some quality time?

'I am using my God-given gifts to extend the kingdom!' But at what cost to your health and your relationships?

'It's only for a season and then things will ease off.' But what if the season never seems to end? How long can you convince yourself and others that it's normal?

'I don't work harder than most people, and not nearly as much as Fred Bloggs in the next-door office.' But who is setting your standard in a culture that has idolised and exalted work above relationships?

'But they couldn't do without me.' The graveyard is full of people who thought that they were indispensable.

4. Do I believe that I have the willpower to stop?   We need to choose to break the cycle of dependence on work. Willpower will not heal the underlying causes. A man may spend more time at home with his family, but if he is still operating out of unmet love needs he is likely to take up a hobby, or some other activity that will keep him occupied at home. We will replace one false comfort with another if we do not deal with the root causes.

5. Are my thoughts increasingly focused on it?   Do you find it hard to leave your work behind at the office, or to concentrate on things other than those related to work? How much of your time away from the place of work is spent planning what to do when you get back there? If you are not able to let it go then it has a stronger hold on you than you may want to admit. Others will feel belittled and unimportant to you. One woman remarked that her workaholic husband was always on another planet and never really listened to her.

Jesus at work

Jesus worked hard, of that there is no doubt. To break free from dependence on work does not mean we don't work overtime or go through periods of intense pressure and activity. Jesus would minister until late in the evening, only to rise early to spend time in prayer. He was often tired and exhausted by his work (Mark 4:38), but as we have seen earlier in this chapter he was never driven by the needs of others or by his own need for human approval and recognition. On the contrary, he was more than happy to be hidden in his work and he would often actively shun the crowds. In John chapter 13 we see the source of his attitude to his work.

> Jesus knew that the Father had put all things under his power and that he had come from God and was returning to God; so he got up from the meal, took off his outer clothing and wrapped a towel around his waist. After that he poured water into a basin and began to wash his disciples' feet, drying them with a towel that was wrapped round him. (John 13:3–5)

The mandate for Jesus' work was first to obey the Father and second to serve the people. He was called to be faithful rather than successful, and was not driven by the need to compete. These two aims were fulfilled as he lived out of an identity that was unshakeably rooted in his relationship with his Father. Jesus knew his Father's approval and blessing. If we have never received the blessing of our earthly fathers we are likely to be striving for success in order to earn their approval or the approval of other authority figures. Do you still look to your parents to praise you for your achievements? If you have given up hope of earning their recognition, do you crave the respect of your peers or your boss?

Adam is a lawyer. He has progressed up the corporate ladder and is very successful in his particular field of company law, but despite his success he feels inadequate and powerless. His answer to these feelings is to pour more time and energy into his work, thinking that it will one day rid him of his personal anxiety. Like so many in his position, Adam never received his father's blessing. As he struggled through adolescence his father never affirmed him in his manhood, and now he has come to see that all his efforts to succeed are his attempt to earn a father's blessing and to prove himself a man. What he cannot get from his own dad, he is now looking for in his boss. He is longing to gain the approval of a father figure. So many men and women are pouring time and energy into seeking the blessing of their bosses and their peers, hoping to find acceptance and recognition. It never works because only God himself is able to reach down into the deepest places of the human heart and impart a solid sense of worth and value.

The Father honoured and trusted his Son by placing all power under his control, but because Jesus' identity was based in a relationship of love, he did not abuse that power. His power was motivated by love and was therefore used to bless others and not exploit them. The man or woman dependent on work is seeking power in one form or another, and that power will end up being used to manipulate the people that they claim to serve. Like Jesus, we need to know our value before the Father, to know where we have come from and where we are going, to know we are born of the spirit and destined for eternity. Only in this way will we be able to work in the world without being tainted and conformed to its standards and values.

Father God, I recognise the real dangers that lie in seeking to find my identity through relationships or achievement. I want to learn to love and be loved and to fulfil my calling to work in your world. Please reveal to me where I have idolised any relationship or any work activity. Give me the grace to break out of wrong patterns of behaviour and to face the pain within me that drives me in these ways. Thank you that you will meet all my needs through Jesus Christ my Lord. Amen.

EXERCISES

1. Do any of your relationships show signs of emotional dependency? Consider the eleven signs and the examples of manipulative behaviour. Are any of these relevant to you?

2. What signs of co-dependency do you recognise in your life? In what ways do you find it hard to identify what is your responsibility and what is not? If your own sense of identity has become merged with someone else's problems, ask yourself the question: 'Whose problem is it?' Having done this, ask the Lord for wisdom about your proper response.

3. How do you respond to failure, to being overlooked or neglected in the work you do? To what degree is your identity found through your achievements and success?

10
Hungry for Love

When I first met Graham he was twenty-eight and single. God was using him in a highly effective ministry, and to all who knew him it seemed that Graham was the happy, healthy and victorious believer that he appeared. However, beneath the surface lurked a strong and seemingly undefeatable lust for sex. Graham was not acting out these desires, he was determined to resist the temptation, but they clouded his imagination and acted like a magnet on his thought life. They induced guilt and shame and undermined his genuine and honest pursuit of an authentic walk with Christ. Because his friends and the other members of his church held him in high esteem, he felt unable to tell them of his secret struggles and therefore his battle with lust served to isolate him from his friends. As a boy Graham had been sent to a boarding school, and while there he began to read the pornography that was so readily available from his friends. His discovery of these magazines coincided with his emerging puberty, and the lustful and graphic sexual images he had looked at were imprinted on his mind and fuelled the increasingly addictive masturbation habit that accompanied them.

When he came into a living relationship with Christ at university, Graham was determined to stop reading pornography. He sought to control the masturbation and to purify his mind and his body. In practice it was much harder than he had anticipated. The desires, thoughts and images would continually assail him, but no matter how hard he tried, no matter how hard he prayed or how many scriptures he memorised, he could not find the purity he was looking for. Whenever he read books or listened to sermons on the subject of sex, no one addressed the reality of what he was battling with. Discouraged by his failure to find victory over his sin, he assumed that his lust was an area in his life that could not be defeated.

The typical dilemma

Graham is typical of so many believers in our culture today. We are besieged by images of sex from the television, the cinema, magazines and even from the advertising boards at the side of the road. Our sexual desires are the object of manipulation by the media, by the advertising moguls, and by large corporations hungry for profit. We live in a society obsessed with sex and the pursuit of personal sexual fulfilment, and yet as we read the Scriptures we see that we are called to live a life of sexual purity:

> But among you there must not be even a hint of sexual immorality . . . [it is] improper for God's holy people. (Ephesians 5:2)

> You have heard that it was said, 'Do not commit adultery.' But I tell you that anyone who looks at a woman lustfully has already committed adultery with her in his heart. (Matthew 5:27)

We know that our bodies are meant to be temples of the Holy Spirit, we know that our minds are meant to be pure and free from lust and sexual imagery, and we know that we should not entertain lustful thoughts and desires. But we do!

The dilemma that so many are facing in the church today is this: we want to be pure and to honour God with our bodies and our minds, but we do not know why we feel the way we do, or what to do with the sinful desires that occupy so much of our time and attention. Graham was stuck in this dilemma, but by the grace of God and with the help of believers who knew how to minister healing he was restored to a place where he was at peace. His mind, imagination and desires were cleansed and purified and he knew a deep-seated freedom from the old compulsions.

Heather was not so lucky. The church she attended taught biblical morality, and though she deeply believed it she still ached for a mate and longed to find the intimacy that she had always hoped for. Sadly no one was able to offer her much more help than a quick prayer and some scriptures that she should hold on to in times of temptation. It was not that this was wrong, but rather that it simply did not go far enough. It did not address the longings of Heather's heart and left her still craving love and tenderness. Heather chose to put her emotional needs before her commitment to obey Christ and she moved in with her boyfriend, who was not a Christian. This resulted in her forsaking her faith and returning to the lifestyle that she had known before her conversion.

Many who know Christ find themselves in this kind of dilemma, and sadly many turn their back on their faith because they cannot find the emotional fulfilment that a sexual relationship appears to offer. Others find themselves vulnerable to secret sexual sin. According to a survey conducted by *Christianity Today*,

12 per cent of pastors admitted to sexual intercourse in the course of pastoral work and 18 per cent had engaged in passionate kissing and petting. Amongst the laity, 45 per cent had done something sexually inappropriate, 23 per cent had sexual intercourse outside of marriage and 28 per cent had engaged in other forms of extramarital sex.[1]

The good news of the gospel is that there truly is grace to satisfy the cry of our hearts, and healing to free us from the control of lustful and addictive sexual desires.

The symbolism of sex

God created us with the ability to enjoy sex as part of the divine mandate to 'be fruitful and increase in number' (Genesis 1:28). Making love is a beautiful part of a marriage relationship, but it is also symbolic of a higher reality. Part of the purpose of the sexual act is to conceive children and to bring forth life. Think for a moment of the imagery involved in this. The woman receives the man within her, in an act of mutual love and trust. The man releases sperm into the woman and together the sperm and egg create a life that is unique and precious. What does this remind you of? This imagery is symbolic of the act of spiritual regeneration. In faith and trust I receive the presence of the Lord within me, and as the Holy Spirit penetrates my human spirit I am born again as a child of God. The intimacy of sex between a man and a woman is an image and symbol of their unity in marriage, and of the even greater intimacy that can exist between the believer and his God.

Paul expresses this deeply mystical aspect of the nature of marriage when he writes: ' "For this reason a man will leave his father and mother and be united to his wife, and the two will become one flesh." This is a profound mystery – I am talking about Christ and the church' (Ephesians 5:31–2).

The one-flesh union in marriage is symbolic not just of the individual believer's spiritual union with God, but also of the relationship of the church with her Bridegroom (Isaiah 62:5; Revelation 19:7, 21:2). God's plan, therefore, is that the sexual act should be kept within the context of a relationship that reflects our relationship with him. Marriage is a covenant relationship for life, to be lived out in mutual love, respect, submission and service (Ephesians 5:21–33).

Satan's plan is always to debase and ruin God's good and perfect gifts. His aim is to split the sexual act from the context of covenant love, and in so doing to damage the souls and bodies of men and women, thereby wounding the heart of God.

> The biblical stress upon relationship helps to enlarge our understanding of human sexuality. The problem with the topless bars and the pornographic literature of our day is not that they emphasise sexuality too much but that they do not emphasise it enough. They totally eliminate relationship and restrain sexuality to the narrow confines of the genital. They have made sex trivial.[2]

Because the act of sex is an image and symbol of a greater reality, Satan's scheme is to fix our human eyes on the symbol while blinding us to the greater reality that lies behind it. He wants us to think continually about the apple that we are not meant to eat, knowing that the more we think about it the more hungry we will become and the more likely we will be to doubt God's good purposes for our lives. As Christians, we must see through these demonic lies and look to the greater reality that all of us who are born of the Spirit, whether single or married, can know the intimacy of the greater spiritual union and be satisfied through our love relationship with Christ. This does not mean that loving, intimate friendships within the body of Christ are not critical to satisfying our God-given desire for companionship and love. We are not spiritual islands that need only God. We need to mediate God's love to each other, but, as we shall see, it is to God that we must look first to satisfy our deepest hunger for love.

Desires that are out of control

Loving relationships are critical to a healthy life. They are a genuine and God-given *need* in each person, and our humanity is diminished if we do not have them in our lives. On the other hand, sexual love is not a *need* but a *want*. Our humanity is not diminished if we are abstaining from sex. The fullest and most perfect expression of humanity was himself a single and celibate individual. The life of Jesus Christ reveals that, while we are all sexual beings, sexuality is a much wider concept than our ability to engage in the genital sex act. In Jesus' life his sex drive was under the control of his will and he expressed his sexuality through being a man who loved God, loved those around him and lived out his humanity in the fullest possible way.

Why then do we who are indwelt by the Spirit and are God's new creations still struggle with such strong desires for sex? One woman expressed this frustration when she asked, 'If God does not want us to have sex before marriage, why then do we want it so much?'

Chastity is the most unpopular of the Christian virtues. There is no getting away from it. The Christian rule is 'either marriage with complete faithfulness to your partner, or else total abstinence'. Now this is so difficult and contrary to our instincts that obviously either Christianity is wrong or our sexual instinct as it now is has gone wrong. One or the other.[3]

As usual, C. S. Lewis puts his finger on the nub of the issue. It is the sexual instinct in the person which has gone wrong, not the Word of God which is at fault. Christ has shown us that it is possible to live a complete life, but with the sexual instinct in its proper place and under control. The need to have the sex drive under control is just as important for a married person as it is for a single person. The sexual act can become the source of great tension, conflict and misery within a marriage if one or both partners are operating out of inappropriate or compulsive sexual desires. Lust does not disappear on the first night of the honeymoon; if it is not dealt with it can continue unchecked and cause great complications within a marriage. Whoever we are and whatever situation we find ourselves in, the time to seek genuine purity and sexual wholeness is now!

Unmet love needs

Neither Graham nor Heather was able to overcome their hunger for sexual intimacy by the use of their will. Graham chose not to act out his desires and fantasies but they still plagued him day by day. Heather did not choose the ways of obedience and withdrew from following Christ. If we are to come to a place of peace and purity, we need to allow the Spirit of God to go to the roots of the problem. We need to allow him to heal the heart in order for our desires to be transformed and our anxious pursuit of love to be quietened.

In ancient Greek there were four different words for love. The first three, *storge*, *philia* and *eros*, are common to all people, but the fourth word, *agape*, is used to express the total self-giving love shown by Christ. It is divine love, lived out by his people in the power of the Spirit. It is helpful to see these four words as being like the four storeys of a house, because in the development of our lives they build on each other; if one of them is damaged it will impact the others.

Storge love

Storge love is the kind of love that a child receives from his parents. A child needs to be filled to overflowing with the power of the storge love that the parent imparts into his love tanks. As we have already seen, this is crucial in the early development of a healthy personality. While we will always need storge love in our lives, the degree to which we are hungry for love in later years will depend on the degree to which we received storge in the critical first stages of life. The first seven years or so are foundational for the rest of our lives. If storge love is generously imparted then the love tanks will be well filled and will establish a strong foundation for life; if not, a lifelong pursuit to fill the tanks will ensue.

```
STORGE
```

Philia love

Philia is the second of the Greek words for love, and relates to friendship love. Philia love builds upon the foundation that storge love has established in the life of the child. A happy and self-confident child is enabled to step out into the world to encounter new relationships and to relate to her peers. It is always fascinating to watch children begin to make friends with each other. They warily circle each other as if coming to terms with the extraordinary fact that there are other little people in the world besides them! This is a time of relating to others and pushing back the boundaries of their experience.

During this period it is quite normal to go through the 'Yuck, boys' or 'Yuck, girls' phase. The sense of solidarity with one's own sex is a strong and healthy aspect in the process of sexual development.

PHILIA
STORGE

Eros love

Philia love builds on storge, and eros builds on them both. Eros takes us all by surprise as suddenly the hormones of puberty kick in and life is changed for ever! All at once our sexual desires start to demand to be noticed and those boys or girls that we had so little time for become the objects of our thoughts and dreams. Having just got used to the nursery slopes, we find ourselves on a black run! But what is going to happen if the first two floors of the building are shaky and unstable? If storge is inadequate, and because philia is insufficient to meet the lack of storge, then sexual love will feel like the answer to our hunger for love.

Unmet emotional needs coupled with the sex drive make a powerful combination. In an age of increasing family breakdown, with the erosion of the sense of community and the loss of morality and sexual discipline, isolated and hurting people are resorting to sex in a disastrous attempt to satisfy their need for love. When a person comes to Christ in this generation they are more likely to have a background of sexual brokenness of one form or another. To tell that person that sex is off limits but not to bring grace and healing to the wounded heart is an inadequate expression of the gospel. We need grace and truth in equal measure to bring the freedom that Christ has won for us. We must go beyond controlling the symptoms and seek to bring healing to the causes of our sexual difficulties. Only in this way will we be able to fulfil Christ's commission to release the oppressed and set captives free (Luke 4:18–19).

We need to see that God never intended our sexual desires to be so strong. It is the result of our own unmet emotional needs, driven by a sexual appetite that has been whipped up to the point of frenzy by a society motivated by the very forces of hell. When our love tanks are healthy and we are walking in the power of the Spirit, we are able to control the drive for sex and live in a place of freedom and peace. In this way we are able to wait until God should lead us into marriage, and then within that marriage express our sexuality in a way that is not needy, manipulative or abusive.

I spoke recently to a mother who has a very beautiful teenage daughter, Sally. Two of Sally's schoolfriends had come to stay. On the way home on the Tube, her friends spent the whole journey talking about sex and the different guys that they fancied on the train. Sally, on the other hand, found their behaviour surprising and rather foolish. That evening she spoke to her mother and asked if it was she who was unusual as she had no strong desire to flirt as her friends had done. Now I know what fantastic parents Sally has. They have well and truly filled her love tanks over the years and have also taught her to understand sex from a godly perspective. Talking to Sally's mother about this incident, I asked about the other two girls. Both of them came from broken homes with absent fathers. They were desperately looking for male affirmation, while Sally, knowing the blessing of her mother and father, did not have the same emotional craving for male attention. This incident clearly portrays the impact of our childhood on our teenage and adult sexuality. Because of her parents' generous love, Sally had full and healthy love tanks, and this emotional stability, coupled with a commitment to live according to biblical truth in the power of the Spirit, enabled her to live with genuine purity and self-control.

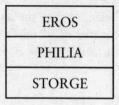

Agape love

Agape love builds on top of the other three storeys. Agape love is unconditional and self-sacrificing love. It is an expression of the heart and also of the will. It is perfectly expressed at the cross, where Jesus laid down his life for the world. 'No greater love [agape] has a man than that he lay his life down for his friends' (John 15:13).

We are able to express agape love as we choose to obey the command and the leading of the Holy Spirit. However, the more we are rooted and established in love, the more complete will be our expression of the love of Christ. When storge and philia have been received in abundance, and if eros is under control, then agape is able to flourish under the anointing of the Spirit. We will truly be able to love one another from the heart.

The cannibal compulsion

Cannibals eat the flesh of the enemies that they respect in order to own and possess the qualities that they would like for themselves. This compulsion is comparable to our hunger for sex, whether it be heterosexual or homosexual. Leanne Payne describes the cannibal compulsion:

> The cannibal compulsion is the twisted way we try to take into ourselves that which we think we lack. In reality it is that within us which (for whatever reason) is unblessed or unaffirmed. In the cannibal compulsion, we are attempting to unite with that unaffirmed facet of our being, or even the sense of being itself. We project the unaccepted part of ourselves off onto another who symbolises that lost part, and then we attempt to swallow it up in that person.[4]

If we are trying to live a pure life, to honour Christ with our eyes, our minds and our bodies, but are still struggling with persistent lustful desires or idealistic romantic fantasies, then there are deeper forces at work within us. We will be exhibiting the cannibal compulsion in some way.

Healing the heart

Understanding the cannibal compulsion was the key to the healing in Graham's life. As a small child he received little touch from his parents and was cared for by a number of different nannies. This lack of physical storge love had left him with separation anxiety and a deep need for a mother's love and touch. Adolescence exposed the inadequacies of his childhood. His love needs became sexualised and the images of women that filled his mind symbolised this deep need to be united with a mother's love. The symbolism in his heart had become very confused, but to a teenage boy it appeared to be the expression of normal adolescent lust. Awakening sexual desires and fantasy life is normal in the adolescent, and does not always involve cannibal compulsions and symbolic confusion. However, in Graham's life the imagery was addictive and compulsive. The masturbation habit that accompanied the diseased imagery and thought life was a sexualised attempt to comfort himself and relieve the deep anxiety that was within him. Where masturbation is a regular habit then it is invariably accompanied by a deep-seated need for comfort and acceptance that is fuelling the compulsion. This is particularly revealed in times of stress or loneliness when many men, and women also, use masturbation to comfort themselves.

At his conversion Graham embraced biblical morality, but without understanding the true nature of his struggles he was unable to take hold of the healing work of the Holy Spirit. In fact, when we first described the cannibal compulsion to him, he could not see how it possibly applied to him. Years of false loyalty to his family had blinded him to seeing any of their deficiencies, and consequently had shut the door to his own healing. Over the following months, God began to open Graham's eyes and reveal his compulsive need to be touched and to be held by a woman. The deep sense of anxiety and abandonment began to surface as he dared to admit that his mother had failed to provide the nurture that he had needed, and we had to stand alongside him in his pain and pray God's love into his innermost being. As we prayed with him and as he learned to look to God on his own, the great exchange began to take place in his heart. He experienced the cleansing work of the cross upon his imagination and desires, and received the imparting of God's love into the 'gaps' within his own heart. God's love imparted to him the love that his

mother had failed to give, and this divine 'mother' love satisfied the hunger of his soul (Isaiah 55:6). The symptoms of his
sexual compulsions were being dealt with, his emotional
needs were being met through the Holy Spirit, and so the
symptoms of his condition began to simply fade away. The
lustful desires, the need to masturbate and the pornographic
images no longer held the power they once had, and as he continued to use his will to choose purity and renounce the old
false comforts he found freedom and release.

Looking beneath the surface

Repentance, prayer and the cleansing work of the Holy Spirit
are likely to be enough to bring a believer to a place of
freedom and purity where the cannibal compulsion is *not*
present. However, many Christians, having done this, still find
that things are not much changed. It is at this point that we
need to look beneath the symptoms to possible root causes.
Once the cannibal compulsion has been discerned, and the
symbolism of the imagery rightly interpreted, then we will be
able to let God minister healing to the root causes of the compulsive desires.

For one person sex may be a means to recover a sense of
power and strength. This macho attitude to sex is particularly
common to unaffirmed men. For another person it may be the
attempt to assuage the aching fear of loneliness. To the woman
who has never received her father's blessing, sex may symbol-
ise the affirmation that she never received. A man with homosexual desires is likely to be seeking to bond with that
masculine part of himself that he was cut off from in childhood. Similarly the woman with lesbian desires may be
hungry for the mother love that she never knew.

This is by no means meant to give simplistic answers to

complex problems, but rather to show that beneath our illicit sexual desires lie emotional roots of love deprivation. Once we can begin to ask the right questions about our struggles then we stand a much greater chance of healing and true freedom.

Because sex is so easily twisted into a means to meet our own needs, and thereby be the very opposite of real love, it is little wonder that God has set such definite boundaries around it. When we try to satisfy our unmet emotional needs through sex, it becomes addictive, manipulative and abusive, and so is a prime tool in the hands of Satan to reap a whirlwind of hurt, oppression and addiction.

The lie of fantasy

Pornography is a retreat into the land of celluloid make-believe by insecure men who are threatened by real women. Feeling inadequate in relating to women with emotions, personality and intelligence, they withdraw into a world of pictures, where their women do whatever they require but demand nothing in return.

Similarly the retreat into the fantasy world of romance, while it looks far less harmful, is just as unrealistic. Romance is all about the drama and excitement of falling in love. Endless books, films and magazines are sold on the basis of our love of romance. Boy meets girl, girl meets boy, they fall in love and live happily ever after. The only problem is that real life does not work like that. Relationships that last are about commitment, hard work and plenty of forgiveness. We are called to live in the present, to live in today, and to give ourselves to the work of loving those people that God has brought our way.

No man is ideal, and no woman is perfect. The danger of

engaging in a romantic fantasy life is that we will come to love the drama of romance more than the person themselves. We will love the flowers, the chocolates, the presents and the attention more than the person who gives them. If I idolise romance, it is because it makes me feel special about myself, and is therefore an expression of unmet emotional needs. Most of us would like a 'living doll' (be it a Barbie or a Ken!) who satisfies our every need, but life is not like that, and the flight into an overdeveloped romantic imagination will only serve to undermine our ability to develop mature relationships that will survive the ups and downs of real life.

Renouncing idolatry

When we look to have our needs met through humans we are engaging in idolatry. We may not be doing so intentionally, but to turn to the creature before the Creator and to look to men or women to meet our deepest needs is idol worship. Wherever there is sexual immorality, there you will find idolatry, and where there is idolatry you will invariably find sexual immorality: 'Therefore God gave them over in the sinful desires of their hearts to sexual impurity for the degrading of their bodies with one another. They exchanged the truth of God for a lie, and worshipped and served created things rather than the Creator' (Romans 1:24–5).

The answer to our longing for intimacy, connectedness, significance and security is not to be found through any man or woman. Heather fell away from Christ because she chose to put a human being first. In reality, she was saying that her man could give her meaning and life more effectively than the living God. She would not have phrased it like that, I am sure, but her actions revealed her unspoken assumptions. Graham, on the other hand, chose to stay upright before the Lord and to resist the great temptation to worship and serve the creation.

It is not until we make a determined attempt to put Christ first and to resist the false comfort of sexual gratification that we will be able to take hold of the deep healing of the Lord. While we are looking to men and women to meet our hunger for love, then we will miss the healing that was purchased at the cross for us all. As we straighten up to God and look to him, resisting the cry of the flesh for satisfaction, then we will be in a position to receive healing and cleansing. It is at this point, as we reach the end of our own resources and look to the Lord to meet our needs, that we will truly feed on him who is the Bread of Life. He will impart love to the empty, fearful and wounded places in our hearts when we eat of him and drink of his Spirit. He will satisfy the hunger of our hearts.

Not only is there healing for the unmet love needs that fuel our inappropriate sexual desires, but there is also healing for the wounds that sexual immorality has caused to our souls and bodies. Cleansing is available for those who have been defiled by others or by their own actions. Shame can be removed and guilt can be forgiven. The restoration of the gospel is available to those struggling with homosexual and lesbian desires. God's salvation is able to restore us, and this includes our sexuality. Graham did not have to live with his compulsions, and neither do you. Healing and grace were available for him; they are also available to you.

There are so many aspects of the healing of our sexuality that I am unable to cover in this one short chapter. My desire is that any who read this and are looking to find a place of purity and freedom in their sexuality will be given hope and an understanding of the emotional forces at work in sexual temptation.

There truly is a place of healing and restoration, no matter how far a person may have fallen or how distorted their sexual desires may have become. Nothing is too hard for the Lord.

> *Father God, I thank you that you are committed to healing and restoring me and bringing me to a place of purity and freedom in my sexuality. You know the ways in which I struggle and the desires and images with which I battle. Thank you that I am forgiven through the blood of Christ and that I am under no condemnation.*
>
> *With your help I determine to live in purity and to resist the pressure of the world around me. I choose today to turn away from seeking the love of humans before your love, and I renounce all idolatry. Please reveal the unmet love needs within me in order that I can allow you to heal and restore my sexuality.*
>
> *I look to you to meet all my emotional needs, through Jesus Christ. Amen.*

EXERCISES

1. Describe your family's attitude towards sex, and the ways in which it has affected you.

   Who were the primary role models that influenced your attitude towards sex? Describe your view of the value and role of sex in a person's life.

2. Describe any aspects of sex or romance in which you are struggling to stay pure and godly.

3. Write out any of the root causes to your present struggles that you are aware of. In what way is the cannibal compulsion present in your life today?

4. Stop and spend time in prayer, asking the Holy Spirit to reveal the root causes of your struggles, and then looking to him to fill you with his perfect love and to meet your unmet emotional needs. Renounce any false worship of men or women.

5. Write down three or four names of people you could possibly share your story and struggles with (they will need to be members of the same sex).

Part 4

THE WAY OF THE SPIRIT

'So I say, live by the Spirit, and you will not gratify the
desires of the sinful nature.' (Galatians 5:16)

11

Seeking the Face of God

As I write, my small daughter is learning to walk. Step by step she is getting the hang of it. Bit by bit she is learning how to keep her balance, and before too long she will have the confidence and skill to totter around the house. There are plenty of bumps but with lots of encouragement she keeps on getting up and going on. The way she learns is by positively focusing on the art of walking, not by concentrating on 'not sitting'! In the same way St Paul's words, 'live by the Spirit and you will not gratify the desires of the sinful nature', are thoroughly positive. He calls us to walk the way of the Spirit, knowing that as we do so we will find that we are no longer succumbing to the influence of the old nature. You do not walk the way of the Spirit by not sinning. You stop sinning by walking the way of the Spirit! Sadly, many Christians spend time and energy focusing on 'not sinning', and in the process miss the abundant grace that could be theirs if they made the way of the Spirit their central aim.

The way of the Spirit is the way of life, truth, power and freedom. It is the only way to maturity and wholeness. Part 4 of this book seeks to show how every single one of us can live by the Spirit in ways that satisfy the deep longings of our hearts and enable the true and real self to grow to maturity. This does not come easily, because our old nature is so used to finding comfort and gratification in things other than God. Just as my daughter has to overcome gravity if she is going to walk, so we too must resist the pull of the old nature and throw ourselves wholeheartedly into learning the way of the Spirit.

A life of prayer

The life of Jesus was saturated with prayer. He prayed when he was alone and when he was surrounded by thronging crowds. He prayed on boats and in the synagogues. He prayed in the mornings and in the evenings. Prayer was the source of his life and his power; it was at the heart of his very existence. The disciples could see this and so they asked Jesus to explain to them the secret of his life of prayer. 'One day Jesus was praying in a certain place. When he finished, one of his disciples said to him, "Lord, teach us how to pray". . . He said to them, "When you pray, say: 'Father . . .'"' (Luke 11:1–2).

The first step in that divine master class on prayer was to learn to call God 'Father'. This is the first and greatest step to take in the life of prayer.

Invited to know the Father

Jesus Christ lived continually in the Father's love. He alone had known the Father since the dawn of time, but now he was intent upon revealing the Father to each of us.

> Righteous Father, though the world does not know you, I know you, and they know that you have sent me. I have made you known to them, and will continue to make you known in order

that *the love that you have for me may be in them* and that I myself may be in them. (John 17:25–6, italics mine)

What an incredible statement! Jesus Christ is drawing every believer into the same love relationship with his Father that he had always known. He is not content that we have a passing acquaintance with the Father. Jesus says that he 'will continue' to make his Father known, in order that the same love that Jesus experienced from his Father would be our experience too. He is determined that we should plumb the depths of the Father's love, just as he has done since before the foundation of the world.

Anyone can say the word 'Father' and anyone can understand the principles of fatherhood. But to actually know the Father is a completely different matter. It is the simplest truth and yet the most profound. To know the Father to the same depth and with the same clarity as Jesus is the highest calling on our lives.

This is the heart of prayer: to learn to be loved by God and to give ourselves in joyful abandonment back to him. When Jesus says that we can call God 'Father', it is not a title with which to address him, but the gateway to a passionate love affair that will consume our hearts and energise the very core of our beings. It is the path to maturity.

The yearning heart of God

The Father loves to meet us heart to heart. He yearns for our love and seeks to draw us to himself, with cords of loving kindness (Hosea 11:4). He has chosen us, saved us and made his home within us, and now he longs that we enjoy precious fellowship with him. He aches with longing for our time, attention and love.

In his book *Good Morning, Holy Spirit*, Benny Hinn recounts an incident that beautifully illustrates this. One evening he was staying in a friend's house while on a ministry trip in England. He was in his room at the top of the house enjoying a particularly intimate and wonderful time with the Lord. Lost in prayer, he heard the woman of the house call up to him, 'Benny, supper is ready.'

As he got up to go downstairs, he felt someone take hold of his hand, and say, 'Five more minutes. Just five more minutes.'[1]

The Holy Spirit longed for his fellowship, and with just the same love and desire he yearns to be alone with you and me. God is jealous for our time and attention. He is not jealous *of* us, but *for* us. Knowing that he is himself the source of all life and blessing, he is jealous for our highest good and he knows that it is to be found in his loving presence.

The prayer cycle

In order to have a full prayer life, we need to understand how different aspects of prayer relate to one another. The cycle of prayer is a helpful tool in doing this.

1. Loving adoration

Prayer begins and ends in loving adoration of the God who has loved us first. The heart of prayer is the prayer of the loving heart. As we learn to seek God for himself, we find that the other aspects of prayer fall into their proper place, and we can be set free from the guilt and striving that blight our prayer lives. As we learn to enjoy God for who he is and not for what we get out of him, our souls and spirits will be deeply satisfied and we will find that our hearts ache to be alone in his presence.

2. *Hearing his voice*

With this intimacy will come a growing ability to hear the voice of the Lord in its many different forms. Listening prayer will bring with it a greater clarity and spiritual wisdom for our lives. We will hear his healing words and receive his blessing day by day. This will then feed directly into the way we intercede and petition the Lord.

3. *Intercession*

To pray 'thy kingdom come, thy will be done' is a crucial element of the life of prayer that every believer is called to participate in: 'I will do whatever you ask in my name, so that the Son may bring glory to the Father. You may ask for anything in my name and I will do it' (John 14:12).

Through prayer we have the great privilege of helping to establish God's will on earth. Cindy Jacobs, a well-known author on prayer, has called us 'God's enforcers' – the people who can bring his will into reality through intercessory prayer! But the key to effective prayer is to have the mind of Christ in the first place. How else can we know what to 'enforce'? A soldier must know his general's commands if he is to play his part in the battle.

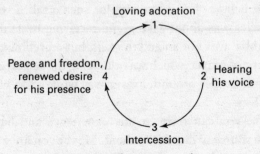

Figure 10 – The prayer cycle

Intercession flows out of intimacy with the Lord. It is a natural overflow of a heart that adores its Creator, for then we are given his heart for the world. It is a tragedy that for so many believers prayer has been reduced to asking for things. At its worst, it is seeking to manipulate God into fulfilling our fleshly desires: 'When you ask you do not receive because you ask with wrong motives, that you may spend what you get on your pleasures' (James 4:3).

At another level, we see worship and adoration as simply the warm-up for the real task of prayer. When I was first ordained, the words of John Wesley's famous phrase motivated my prayer life: 'God has bound himself to do nothing except in answer to prayer.' I believed that if I was not covering all that went on with prayer then I was failing in my role as a minister. I took upon my shoulders a false responsibility and felt driven to pray. Prayer became a burden. I lost intimacy with the Lord in my confusion and soon I was striving in my own strength. I felt like Atlas, who carried the world upon his shoulders, except that I was carrying the kingdom of God! Because I was not operating from a place of intimacy I had not heard his instructions for prayer and therefore I was moving in human wisdom and strength.

Like a great many Christians, the teaching that I received as a young believer had set me up for such a fall. I was taught that prayer was about asking and receiving by faith. To call God 'Abba' was not an end in itself, but a preliminary to the real work of prayer, which was changing the society and influencing the people around. Prayer was work and I was on the payroll!

Maybe you can relate to my experience and have found prayer a source of discouragement. Maybe you are wearied by it and feel guilty for evading opportunities to pray. One of the primary reasons that Christians struggle with prayer is that they have stepped into the circle of prayer at the wrong point. Instead of being a source of intimacy and love, it starts as a job of work to be done. A wonderful old saint used to begin his times of prayer in one of two ways: either he would say, 'Lord, I come to you as a lover,' or, 'Lord, I come to you to do business.' When we confuse these two forms of prayer we are sure to end up striving, guilty and weighed down by the very thing that should breathe life and joy into our hearts.

Once I saw my mistake, God's way of sorting me out was to tell me to stop praying and to start loving. I was about to be turned upside down! I had to break my mindset of prayer as an activity and learn to see prayer as a way of being. This was very hard to do because it went directly opposite to my deeply held beliefs. Looking back on that time I do so with immense gratitude. As I have learned to 'waste time' in his presence, I have grown in my ability to love and be loved. He has become more real to me and I have come to know him in much greater depth. Healing and restoration have been poured into the gaping holes in my own soul and I have learned to taste of his goodness and mercy in a deeper way. I no longer have to strive to cover everything in prayer, but have learned to wait on the Spirit for his direction and wisdom. I am now able to pray with greater simplicity and, I hope, with greater effect. I am learning to pray the prayers that he prays through me.

4. Renewed desire for him

Once intercession flows out of love and trust, then we can live in confidence and peace, and this increases our desire to run into his presence and be alone with him. No longer is prayer a burden imposed by a hard taskmaster, but the precious gift of a loving Father.

This is what I have come to call the circle of prayer, which is a reflection of the priorities revealed in the Lord's Prayer. As we learn to pray according to the Master's way, prayer is restored to its rightful place as the source of life and joy for every child of God.

Dependence

The first step in prayer is to come in weakness and need to the source of all life and grace. Our hearts are so well shielded by our attempts at self-protection that we do not quickly see our great need. Pride and independence go hand in hand. Because of our pride we go astray and miss the grace of God. 'God resists the proud, but gives grace to the humble' (1 Peter 5:5).

The more we allow God to humble us, the more we will rely on his grace rather than our own wisdom or strength. Our society teaches us to rely on ourselves, but we must unlearn these lessons and come naked and needy into the presence of God. Only there will we discover our true identity. This is clearly a lesson that Archbishop Desmond Tutu has learned:

> Usually I get up early in the morning. I try to centre myself on God so that He influences the rest of my day. Many times this is a difficult thing to do. During part of this time I kneel and then I crouch almost like a foetus. There is something about becoming a baby in the presence of God. Being embraced . . . and being made to know that you are special, precious and loved. It's not because I can rush into Lesotho and out again, and appear on television; it's not because I am an archbishop that gives me worth. Worth comes as a gift from God, free of charge. I have gradually come to accept this.[2]

Until we are able to freely acknowledge our need before Almighty God, until we can be like tiny dependent children who cannot survive by themselves, we will never be able to receive the grace to meet God heart to heart. Once we learn to accept this it becomes a source of great relief and joy. We can begin to delight in our weakness as an opportunity to know God at a new and deeper level. Dependence is the beginning of true prayer and the end of it.

> More than anything else, it is the loving contemplation of its Maker that causes the soul to realise its own insignificance, and fills it with holy fear and true humility.[3]

Solitude

Having fed the five thousand, Jesus found himself in a position of great power. The people wanted to make him king. Here at last was a man with the power to meet their every need! But Jesus' response is quite unexpected: 'Jesus, knowing that they intended to come and make him king by force, withdrew again to a mountain by himself' (John 6:15).

Jesus literally fled the crowds to be alone with his Father. The pursuit of worldly power sickened him and he was having nothing to do with it. His answer was to find some solitude in the midst of his pressurised life. It was his custom to find a place far from the needs and cries of the people and spend time with his Father. He taught that we should do the same: 'But when you pray, go into your room, close the door and pray to your Father, who is unseen. And your Father, who sees what is done in secret, will reward you' (Matthew 6:6).

Jesus is deeply concerned with our secret lives. What we do, what we say and what we think when no one else is around reveal what we are truly like. It is in this place of solitude that we will find that the masks that we put up in public begin to come down. We will start to reveal ourselves to God because we can dare to admit, to him and to ourselves (which is often much harder), what we are really like. When there is no one to impress and no one to be frightened of, when we are free from all the pressure of our peers or our parents, we can venture out from behind our walls to find acceptance, cleansing and help in the presence of God.

The section on false comforts reveals how we try to find security and meaning through destructive and manipulative patterns of behaviour. We must be alone with God in order for him to reveal to us our addiction to the world and the opinions of men. Alone with God we have nothing to lean on but his presence, no voice to listen to but his, and no purpose to fulfil but to love and be loved. By doing this we allow him to restore to us our true humanity. True humanity is found in our ability to love God and then to love our neighbour.

Jacob – the man who wrestled with God

From his birth Jacob was a crook, always on the look-out for the main chance. His very name means 'he deceives'. He stole his brother's blessing from Isaac, their father, and from that moment on he was off and running. Not only did he run from his brother Esau, but he ended up running from God. Jacob lived by his wits and through dishonest business practices became a rich man. After many years he finally returned to meet the brother he cheated. Jacob sent the family and the servants ahead of him to meet his brother first, and he remained alone to follow on the next day: 'So Jacob was left alone, and a man wrestled with him till daybreak' (Genesis 32:24).

It was God himself who had come to meet Jacob. Jacob had nowhere to go, nowhere to hide. God met him when he was alone.

Then the man said, 'Let me go for it is daybreak.'

But Jacob replied, 'I will not let you go unless you bless me.'

The man asked him, 'What is your name?'

'Jacob,' he answered.

Then the man said, 'Your name will no longer be Jacob, but Israel.' (Genesis 32:26–8)

In the solitude God met with Jacob, and after wrestling all night Jacob cried out for a blessing. He admitted his need, knowing that the only blessing he had ever received had been a stolen one. But before he could receive it he had to confess his name: Jacob – 'Deceiver'. Once he had admitted his nature and his need, God was ready to change him and give him a new name. From that moment onwards he was a different man, he was Israel.

Solitude causes us to face our own brokenness and addictions. Solitude is painful. Solitude is revealing. The more we run from being alone, the more we need to seek it. Solitude is critical if we are to encounter God in the depths of our soul. Once we have learned to value solitude and meet the Lord in it, we will no longer be driven by our need for human approval or affirmation.

Because Christ found his identity in the Father's love he had no desire for the applause of the crowds. He sought intimacy with the Father above the praise of the people.

Silence

It is quite possible to be alone with God and to protect yourself from actually encountering him. Sometimes this is intentional, but most often we do not know we are doing it. As God began to transform my prayer life I realised that I used words to control my times with God. The true end of all worship and confession is silence. I saw that the words I used in prayer, in praise and confession, well-intentioned as they were, did in fact keep God at arm's length. I had to learn how to be quiet! More than that, I had to learn how to be still.

> Be still before the Lord . . . because he has roused himself from his holy dwelling. (Zechariah 2:13)

> Be still, and know that I am God. (Psalm 46:10)

To be still is to hand over control and to acknowledge our smallness and weakness. Without silence there can be no true humility.

We are so used to noise in our society that silence feels utterly deafening until we get used to it. We can feel disorientated without words to read or noise to hear. There is a time for stillness and a time for words; just as there are times for lovers to have long silent hugs, so there are times for intense discussion.

As we learn to rest, to seek peace and to quieten our anxious hearts and minds, we allow our hearts to wait expectantly for the Lord. Not primarily for what he would speak to us, nor for directions for life, but for a deeper awareness and intimate knowledge of the Lord himself. We do not need something cognitive from God to justify our times of stillness and silence.

Silence allows our hearts to be suffused with light as we eagerly and expectantly press towards him in love. In silence we wait in faith for the Lord to reveal himself in love. The effectiveness of our stillness cannot be measured by the level of sensory experience of God's presence. Sometimes we are aware of him and other times we are not. We walk by faith and not by sight or emotions. We rest in his presence because he who is the Unseen Real is present to our hearts, and we trust his promise that he will draw near to those who draw near to him (James 4:8).

In the silence we allow the storms that rage in our hearts to manifest themselves. This is painful, for silence allows all sorts of desires and images that we work so hard to suppress to rise up into consciousness. This must be allowed to happen, however unpleasant it may be. This kind of prayer allows the sickness of the soul to be revealed, forgiven and healed. The rest and tranquillity that we seek comes only through the purging fire of the Spirit. In silence we surrender ourselves to God and allow him complete freedom into the very depths of the soul.

Beholding

Let us fix our eyes on Jesus. (Hebrews 12:1)

In the stillness of our solitude we gaze with the 'eyes of the heart' upon the very person of God himself. It is not that we see him with our human eyes, or even that we have some image of him in our imaginations, but rather the heart receives spiritual revelation and assurance of his loving presence. As the author of *The Cloud of Unknowing* wrote, 'By love he can be caught and held, but by thinking never.' It is like being aware of someone you love being close at hand, though you may not be able to see them.

We cannot force love or make it happen according to our planned agenda. All we can do is place ourselves in the way of his love and wait in simple trust and dependence. If we were looking for an easy and simple way to pray we would not choose this way. Simple solutions to prayer are invariably superficial and shallow. In reality contemplative prayer, with its emphasis on silence and solitude, is the simplest form of prayer, but we sophisticated moderns have lost the art of still-ness and simplicity. We have lost the way of the heart and have resorted to talking about God rather than meeting him in the depths of our souls.

> Now the Lord is the Spirit, and where the Spirit of the Lord is, there is freedom. And we, who with unveiled faces all reflect the Lord's glory, are being transformed into his likeness with ever-increasing glory, which comes from the Lord, who is the Spirit. (2 Corinthians 3:17–18)

Feeding upon his life

When we celebrate the sacrament of communion, we are entering into the deep symbolism of Christian reality. We come in humility upon our knees to receive the bread and the wine. This symbolises not only the death of Christ and all that he has won for us on the cross, but also the life of Christ. He who is alive now dwells within us and as we partake of the body and the blood we receive his life within us afresh. He is the Bread of Life. He is the New Wine of the kingdom. As we feed on his abundant life we are filled and renewed. Our souls are satisfied by his presence and energised by his goodness.

This symbolism of the Eucharist reveals to us the need for every man and woman to learn to feed on the life of Christ. We need his life every day and every moment. As we seek to behold the face of God in times of intense and uninterrupted prayer, so we are enabled to practise his presence throughout the day.

> The practice of the Presence is the discipline of calling to mind the truth that God is with us. When we constantly do this, the miracle of seeing by faith is given, and we begin to see with the eyes of the heart.[4]

As we grow in our grace-given ability to behold him with our hearts, we are able to feed on his life in each and every situation. We allow his life to pierce the darkness and bring light, healing and strength. We learn to 'know the love that surpasses knowledge' as his perfect love ministers to the deep needs in our hearts. Our wounded hearts begin to fill with his love.

Once we have learned to do this behind closed doors, we can do it anywhere. In the most pressurised of situations we can always enter that still and trusting place in our hearts that has been developing in the times of solitude. With hungry hearts and faith-filled expectation we turn to him and allow him to impart life to us.

As we feed on Christ in this way, he heals and restores us. Before too long, if we have learned to persist in prayer, we come to realise that the old fears and compulsions have begun to disappear and where there once was insecurity and inadequacy, sin and addiction, now there is his life, power, purity, confidence and love: 'So I say, live by the Spirit and you will not gratify the desires of the sinful nature . . . The fruit of the Spirit is love, joy, peace, patience, kindness, goodness, faithfulness, gentleness and self-control' (Galatians 5:16–22).

The best counselling, the greatest teaching, the most vibrant church, the closest of friendships cannot impart to us the life of Christ by themselves. Christ alone can impart life to us at these deep places in our souls. We have to meet him ourselves. Alone, vulnerable and in the silence. There we will prove the faithfulness and love of God. There we will embrace the work of transformation that must be wrought in our souls. There we will come to love him with an undying passion, for we will have met with the living God and found that he is the fulfilment of our heart's deepest desires.

Twenty-first-century pilgrims

We are all called to grow into the likeness of Christ, and therefore we are all on a pilgrimage. The journey is one in which we press 'farther up and farther in' as we seek the face of the Lord. Space prohibits me writing about the mechanics of contemplative prayer; however, I would highly recommend Jim Borst's book, *Coming to God in the Stillness*. It is very practical and deeply profound, and God has used it to lead me into a deeper and more intimate prayer life.

In today's society everyone is offering ten easy steps to this or the shortest route to that but I can offer no fast-food answer to prayer. Just as with any committed relationship, knowing and being known, loving and being loved, are the work of a lifetime. The same is true of prayer. Prayer that seeks the face of God and dares to be truly self-revealing will be rewarded. You will reap what you sow.

> Then your Father, who sees what is done in secret, will reward you. (Matthew 6:6)

> You will seek me and find me when you seek me with all your heart. (Jeremiah 29:13)

The more we behold his presence and taste his love, the more we will want to be alone with him. God yearns for us with intense desire, and as we respond with open hearts to seek his face, his life will flood our souls, we will grow in maturity and the true self born of the Spirit will emerge to give glory to God.

Father God, thank you that you have put within me a deep desire to know you heart to heart. I ask you to increase that desire within me.

Please impart to me a greater revelation of yourself.

Open the eyes of my heart that I might behold you and adore you. Teach me to be still in your presence, to 'waste time' alone with you, and to allow you to penetrate the darkness within my soul.

I choose to seek you with all my heart, knowing that you are the fulfilment of my deepest desires and the answer to the cry of my heart. Amen.

EXERCISES

1. What motivates you to pray?

    Choose the words that best reflect your motivation to pray: fear, anxiety, love, guilt, habit, pressure to perform, fervent desire, need, to know the will of God, to bring the chance to others . . . (please add your own).

    What influences have led you to be motivated in this way?

2. Consider the prayer cycle. How do the different aspects relate to one another in your own prayer life?

3. How do you handle solitude?

    What do you feel at the prospect of spending a significant length of time alone with God? How long do you think you could handle at the moment?

    What does this say about you? (Please do not judge yourself!)

    What does this say about your view of God?

4. Spend fifteen minutes alone with God in silence. The following may be helpful:
    (a) Seek to rest and relax in his loving presence.
    (b) When your thoughts or other noises invade the silence,

acknowledge them and then let them go. Write down anything you need to remember to do later.

Commit fears and worries into God's safekeeping. Return to your steady focus on the Lord.

Quieten your heart. Be still and alert.

Confess lustful thoughts, anger or hatred and compulsive desires to the Lord. Thank him that you are forgiven.

(c) Open yourself to an awareness of God's presence with you.

Surrender yourself completely.

(d) Gaze upon him with the eyes of your heart. Seek him in love.

(e) Rest in his presence. Do not analyse yourself; just 'be'.

Waste time. Do not look for feelings or new understanding to justify your time with him.

(f) Finish by thanking him.

12

Truth that Sets Us Free

> Then Jesus was led by the Spirit into the desert to be tempted by
> the devil. After fasting for forty days and forty nights, he was
> hungry. The tempter came to him and said, 'If you are the Son of
> God, tell these stones to become bread.' Jesus answered, 'It is
> written: "Man does not live on bread alone, but on every word
> that comes from the mouth of God."' (Matthew 4:1–4)

After forty days in the desert, Jesus was more hungry to obey
the Word of God than he was to eat bread. He was utterly
committed to living under the Word, because it brought life.
Though he himself was the Word of God, he willingly chose
to humble himself and become obedient to the Scriptures and
the voice of the Father. Because he lived *under* the truth, Jesus
was able to speak *out* the truth: 'The words I have spoken to
you are spirit and they are life' (John 6:63).

If we are to embrace life, then we too must learn to live by
the Word of God. If the Word of God was so crucial to Christ,
how much more crucial it is to us who are so deeply influenced
by the materialism and humanistic wisdom of our age.

The battle for reality

There is a battle being waged for the right to define reality. Satan's plan is to control the thoughts and manipulate the mindset of every nation and every individual. If he can deceive the peoples with his lies, then the strongholds that he establishes at the levels of the society, the family and the individual make them more resistant to the power of the gospel.

> The god of this age has blinded the minds of unbelievers, so that they cannot see the light of the gospel of the glory of Christ, who is the image of God. (2 Corinthians 4:4)

Once a person is born again of the Spirit, Satan's strategy is to deceive them into a life of compromise in which they allow the strongholds to remain intact, thereby giving him opportunity to influence their behaviour. We succumb to this deception when we allow the 'words' of our society, our family and our peers to determine our perception of reality.

Reality can be defined as *that which is true, that which has objective existence and to which we conform our lives.*

> The essence of spiritual warfare is in what shall define reality: the Word of God or the illusions of the present age.[1]

It is only as we learn to perceive the reality of the Word of God that we enter into the mind of Christ, and it is only as we live it out that we enjoy true freedom.

> If you hold to my teaching, you are really my disciples, then you will know the truth and the truth will set you free. (John 8:31)

God's Word brings:

Truth   John 17:17
Light   Psalm 119:130

Life   John 6:63
Freedom   John 8:31

Satan's word brings:

Deception   1 Timothy 4:1
Darkness   Romans 1:21
Death   John 10:10
Bondage   Ephesians 2:1–3

What defines your self-image? Is it the Word of the Lord, or the words that your parents or your peers have spoken over you? What defines your moral standards? Is it the standards of Scripture or the ways of our society? How do you plan your life? Is it in submission to the directions of the Holy Spirit or do you expect God to bless the plans that you make on your own? Whose word do you *really* live by?

Perhaps the most crucial question in our lives is: 'Am I truly prepared to conform my life to God's Word and allow the Spirit to reveal anything and everything that is in rebellion against him?'

The choice really is as stark as that. To believe or to do something that is contrary to the Word of God is to be in rebellion against God. To water down truth means that we are casual about holiness and content to allow sin a place in our lives. We must conform our lives to his truth, or else we will oppose God in those areas where our strongholds have not been demolished. This is the way of spiritual deception and hypocrisy. Once we begin to 'take every thought captive for Christ', we will find that our emotions and habits begin to change and we are freed from the manipulation and domination of the world, the flesh and the devil.

Cry out to God. Now. This very minute. Implore him to send the Spirit of truth to shine his light upon your mind and upon your heart. Receive him by faith and be fully prepared to face the consequences.

The impact of the Word

The Word of God impacts our lives at three key levels.

1. *The Word brings revelation of God*

Alex closed his eyes and said, 'If God was in the next room, I think he would be a judge. It would be a frightening thing to imagine him coming to meet me.' Alex's mother had tried to abort him and his twin and though the other child had died, Alex had survived. A deep primal fear had been lodged in his heart from that moment onwards, and now was being projected on to the character of God. Alex was a missionary, a man steeped in the Scriptures, but at a heart level he only knew God from a distance. He had almost no real understanding of God as a loving father.

A. W. Tozer wrote:

> What comes into our minds when we think about God is the most important thing about us. The history of mankind will probably show that no people has ever risen above its religion, and man's spiritual history will positively demonstrate that no religion has ever been greater than its idea of God. Worship is pure or base as the worshipper entertains high or low thoughts about God.[2]

Without the Word of God we would all project on to God our own fears, lusts, hopes and desires. The Greeks had gods that were promiscuous, warlike, vengeful and fickle. Left to ourselves, we too would create gods little better than the Greeks', and maybe a lot worse. But Christianity is a revealed faith. God has made himself known to us through the written Word, through Christ the living Word and through his creation. It is the work of the Holy Spirit to open our minds and hearts to his nature and character; as we allow the written Word to impart truth to us we begin to perceive God as he really is, and the living Word dwells more fully within us. Through the healing work of the Spirit and the revelatory work of the Word, Alex has come to know God as a loving father, a faithful friend and a righteous judge. His walk with God is intimate yet filled with reverence and awe. The Word of God, energised by the Spirit, has brought him revelation, peace and freedom.

2. The Word brings wisdom

Wisdom is not the same as information. Wisdom is a deep understanding of the ways of God and is foundational for a life that is pleasing to God. Though God has imparted his holiness to us, we will not live it out unless our minds and hearts are being soaked in his truth. Solomon wrote Proverbs to impart wisdom to the people:

> The proverbs of Solomon son of David, king of Israel:
> for attaining wisdom and discipline;
>   for understanding words of insight;
> for acquiring a disciplined and prudent life,
>   doing what is right and just and fair. (Proverbs 1:1)

God promises to impart wisdom to those who lack it (James 1:5) but this is not some magical gift. It is given as the Spirit of God opens our hearts to the wisdom of the Word and enables us to live it out. Wisdom is a gift from God, but it only comes as we saturate our lives with the truth.

3. *The Word brings personal growth*

It is critical for a child to receive words that bless and encourage. Words of affirmation bring forth the gifts, the personality and the true hopes and desires that are within the developing child and adolescent. Without these words of life we fail to become all we were made to be.

Stored in our hearts are the words that others have spoken over us throughout our lives. Some of these words may have been life-giving and affirmed us in our identity, while others may still act as chains that bind us and prevent us growing and changing. Our minds and hearts are like cassette tapes that keep playing back the words that have been spoken to us. We need to keep those that have blessed us, but wipe out those that have cursed our lives. Choosing to believe and receive God's words of life deep into our hearts, we will begin to break the power of those thoughts and words that have been destructive. We then look to God's Word to establish our identity and self-image. Under the blessing of our loving Father we can become all that he has made us to be. We can walk in godly confidence and security because we have heard him speak life and blessing to us.

As a teenager I experienced great pain and rejection at the hands of my peers, whose physical and verbal bullying tore my self-worth and self-esteem to shreds. Because I was at boarding school, I did not have my parents to turn to and no other adult took their place, so I was bereft of blessing and affirmation. The healing of my heart and the restoration of self-esteem has come about through much grace and plenty of hard work. I have had to consciously identify, reject and renounce the destructive words that I had come to believe about myself. In their place I have had to consciously receive and believe the words of blessing that my heavenly Father has imparted to me. Mostly these words have come from Scripture, but others have come through listening prayer.

In the areas where I have needed God's blessing, I have had to hold on to the Word. When the feelings of inadequacy have risen up in me and I have withered under their intensity, I have held on to Ephesians 2:10 with all my might: 'For we are God's workmanship, created in Christ Jesus for good works, which God prepared in advance for us to do.' Holding on to this scripture, meditating on it and speaking it out has been critical in enabling my deep heart to believe that I am God's workmanship – his beloved masterpiece. I am not inadequate, weak or shameful but gifted, anointed and empowered by God. Standing on this truth, this understanding of reality, I have been able to resist the assault of Satan as he has used the old destructive words to try and prevent me changing. God's Word is not dry and dusty but the channel by which we are able to receive life-imparting truth into the wounded and broken areas of our lives. When our emotions and desires are assaulting us and urging us to do or to think that which is contrary to God's truth, then we have to draw on the Word of God and the power that it releases in our lives.

In times of loneliness, fear, anxiety, insecurity, despair, it is the Word of God that will be our anchor and will keep us rooted in truth. Through his Word he will feed us and empower us to live fully and become conformed to the image of his Son, the living Word, who dwells within us.

How to do it

If we are to live by the Word of God, then we need to embrace certain fundamental principles.

Study the Word

Millions of words have been written in the Western world about the way to study the Bible. I do not want to add to them here. Learning to study the Scriptures is not very hard once one understands the basic steps. With the help of concordances, commentaries and Bibles with modern texts, learning to study the Word is easier than it has ever been. The real issue lies in our motivation. In an age of relativistic thinking and the pursuit of pleasure, will we choose to transcend the culture and learn to think biblically?

> You were taught, with regard to your former way of life, to put off your old self, which is being corrupted by its deceitful desires; to be made new in the attitude of your minds, and to put on the new self, created to be like God in true righteousness and holiness. (Ephesians 4:22–4)

Unless the attitude of our minds is being transformed and conformed to the truth, we will never be able to put on the new self. We will remain in deception and bondage, living out of compulsive desires and fears.

Memorise the Word

When Jesus was tempted in the desert, he did not dust off his Torah to find a relevant verse of Scripture. The Word was already in his heart. Because he had memorised it, he was able to bring its life and power to bear on the temptation that he was facing. As we study the Word, we need to memorise those truths that are relevant for our lives and which help us demolish our strongholds. This does not mean memorising a chapter at a time, but rather those verses that the Spirit highlights. The more we memorise Scripture, the easier it becomes. The key is to start!

Begin by writing out the verse once or twice, and then speaking it out without looking at it. Then think about something else, and after a moment or two, recall the verse from your memory. In this way you will learn to find it in your memory banks. The more you think on the verse, the more it will become ingrained in your memory.

Meditate on the Word

Having memorised the portion of Scripture, you are now in a position to let its power be unleashed in your life. The next step is to meditate on it. The purpose of meditation is to allow the truth and the power of the Word to be established in your inner being: 'I have hidden your word in my heart that I might not sin against you' (Psalm 119:11).

It is not enough to simply know a scripture in the mind. Until it has become established in the inner being it will not empower us to live it out. The concept behind meditation is that of a cow chewing the cud. As a cow eats, it chews the grass again and again until it has extracted from it all the nutrients. In the same way the mind and the heart are able to suck life out of God's Word as we chew on it. To know Scripture in the mind but not to meditate on it is like tasting good food but never swallowing it. Meditating on the Word allows the Spirit the opportunity to bring revelation to your innermost being.

If we do not learn to meditate on the Word our strongholds will remain intact. The answer to breaking the power of the lies we have believed is to take hold of God's liberating and life-changing Word. Books, sermons, tapes and articles may enable us to perceive new truths, but until we have made them our own through meditation we will be in danger of falling back into the old habits and attitudes.

I often meditate on John's vision in Revelation 4:1–6, where John describes the throne of God in pictorial language. This meant nothing to me while I analysed the vision with my rational mind and divided it into different truths about God. But once I started to let my imagination picture the scene that John is painting, I was gripped by the majesty and grandeur of God. I began to develop a deep sense of awe and wonder in his presence. Much of the language of Scripture is pictorial and intended to capture the imagination. We must not be afraid to use our imaginations to picture what is described in the Word. That is what the writers wanted us to do, in order that the imagery that they were depicting would impart truth to our hearts.

When we meditate on a verse that is a rational statement, then we need to allow the heart and mind to contemplate the significance of each and every word. In this way we open the door between the head and the heart.

Meditating on Scripture also releases faith. Faith is not a feeling, but a settled conviction that God is true to his Word. As we feed on the Word the Spirit causes the faith to rise within us: 'Faith comes from hearing the message, and the message is heard through the word of Christ' (Romans 10:16).

If you want to grow in faith, don't stand around waiting for it to happen: press into the Word, meditate on the promises and character of God, and faith will grow within you. Our faith is in his faithfulness and his faithfulness is revealed through his Word.

Pray the Word

As we meditate on the Word the most natural thing to do is to breathe the Word back to him. As I meditated on Ephesians 2:10, I began to thank God that *I* was *his* workmanship. As I thanked him faith and joy rose within me and I began to believe it in my heart. I would also ask the Father for a greater revelation of this truth so that I might be more rooted and grounded in the knowledge of his delight and pride in me. Over time this has become reality to me, so that the old lies that I once viewed as truth no longer have a hold on me.

When we pray the Word, it is important that we learn to speak it out loud. This is more than just a technicality. Joshua was commanded: '*Do not let this Book of the Law depart from your mouth*, meditate on it day and night, so that you may be careful to do everything that is written in it. Then you will be prosperous and successful' (Joshua 1:8, italics mine).

Joshua was to keep the Word in his mouth, or in other words he was to speak it out. At one level it is helpful to speak out the Word, because hearing it and thinking it makes it easier to memorise. However, there is a deeper reason which relates to the nature of the Word of God.

The Word of God is exactly that. It is the expression of God's very nature. The Word is true because God himself is truth. The Word is eternal because God himself is eternal. When God's eternal and unchanging Word is spoken into the temporal and changing realm then the creation is conformed to his Word. God spoke at creation and his Word established the universe. 'By the word of the Lord were the heavens made . . . For he spoke, and it came to be; he commanded, and it stood firm' (Psalm 33:9).

It is this principle that is demonstrated in Jesus's ministry. When he spoke healing to a body, the tissue conformed to his command. When he spoke life to the dead, death gave up its captives. The source of the power is in his Word. As we learn to hear God's Word through the Scriptures and then speak it out in faith, we begin to live as a prophetic people.

This dynamic is a spiritual law and operates as surely as a

physical law. It is applicable to the way we intercede for the world, but also for ourselves. As I speak out God's Word into the areas of my life that do not yet conform to it (fear, anxiety, sickness, inadequacy . . .) I will be sowing life and truth which will bring forth a harvest in the days ahead. As I resist the assault of the enemy using the Word of God, then I will be wielding the sword of the Spirit as God intended. As I stand my ground and live according to the Word, Satan will have to flee. He trembles at the Word far more than at our good intentions or human wisdom. We give up too easily, not understanding that it takes perseverance and faith to see change and transformation. If we sow the seed of the Word in faith, we will reap the harvest (Galatians 6:7–10).

Do the Word

When did you last hold a tadpole in your hand? They have such huge heads and such little bodies! Despite all our learning, our theological colleges and biblical knowledge, the Western church has so little power or impact. We are like the tadpoles. We have great learning, but we do not live it out. Our heads are big, but our bodies are puny. The early church was the opposite. They had little theology and were learning as they went, but they lived out what they knew. Obedience, determination, prayer and the power of the Spirit were the keys to their success. Jesus said: 'Blessed . . . are those who hear the word of God and obey it' (Luke 11:28).

There is no substitute for obedience. When asked the secret for his life, Pastor Yonggi Cho replied, 'I pray a lot and I obey a lot!' Biblical knowledge must be converted into action or else we will fall into deception. 'Do not merely listen to the word and so deceive yourselves. Do what it says' (James 1:22).

Spiritual maturity

Spiritual maturity is defined by our likeness to Christ. As we look at his life we see him steeped in the Scriptures, but we also see him listening to his Father for specific directions: 'I do nothing on my own but speak just what the Father has taught me. The one who sent me is with me; he has not left me alone' (John 8:28–9).

Not only did Jesus not speak any words that the Father had not taught him, but he did not do anything that the Father did not show him to do: 'I tell you the truth, the Son can do nothing by himself; he can do only what he sees his Father doing, because whatever the Father does the Son also does' (John 5:19).

Our ability to hear the voice of the Lord and to see the will of the Father is critical to living a mature and effective Christian life.

Words of love

The Spirit whispers words of love to us. He affirms us and blesses us in the most beautiful of ways as we learn to be intimate with him. When God began to shake my stronghold of pride and self-sufficiency, I felt very vulnerable and unprotected. I realised that my need for success masked my real feelings of weakness and inadequacy. As I was praying about this, the Holy Spirit showed me a picture of a large warrior running through the jungle. His strength and power were obvious and he was ready for battle. God spoke to my heart and said, 'This is how I see you, Stuart.' I was profoundly impacted by this word. If that was how God saw me, then that was the truth and why should I care what anyone else thought? I can only describe the revelation in inadequate words, because the picture and the words imparted something of the warrior's strength and power into my heart. From then on I would meditate on the picture whenever I was in need of strength or felt inadequate. I was learning to see myself from God's perspective.

Listening prayer

The prophet Habakkuk gives us an insight into his way of hearing God that is very practical and helpful:

> I will stand at my watch . . .
> I will look to see what he will say to me . . .
> Then the LORD replied: Write down the revelation.
>   (Habakkuk 2:1–2)

1. I will stand at my watch

Each one of us needs a place where we regularly go to seek the face of the Lord and to listen to him. We too must stand at our watch ready to hear his Word.

2. I will look to see

We can come with expectation knowing that he is a father who loves to speak to his children.

3. I will look to see what he will say to me

We come prepared for the Lord to communicate to us in whatever way he chooses. The Holy Spirit uses our human faculties for receiving communication as the means to speak to us. Thus pictures, words, feelings and sounds (stimuli which the body receives and the brain interprets) are used by the Holy Spirit as channels into our consciousness. This may, for example, take the form of:

- *pictures* planted in the imagination (dreams, Matthew 2:22; visions, Acts 10:10);
- *words or thoughts* planted into the mind (audible voice, Acts 9:4; inner voice, Acts 13:13);
- *feelings or physical sensations* (an intuitive sense or deep knowing, Mark 2:8);
- *spiritual sounds* that convey meaning (heard audibly, 1 Kings 18:41; or with the 'inner' ear).

There really is nothing mystical or strange about hearing the Word of the Lord. At the heart of the Bible is the revelation that God is a speaking and communicating God. We who are born of the Spirit are all able to hear God speak to us today. We need to listen to the voice of the Spirit while becoming rooted in his Word. These two ways of hearing God are not in opposition to each other, as long as we submit anything we sense God has spoken to us beneath the standard of his written Word.

The mystery and wonder lie in the fact that the holy and wise God should want to trust us with his words in the first place! But trust us he does if we will come with open hearts, listening ears and a willingness to be obedient. I would love to spend time unpacking the different ways God speaks to us, but this book is not intended to cover everything in detail. A study of the references given above will be helpful, but I recommend that you read in more detail if these concepts are new to you.

4. The Lord replied, 'Write down the revelation'

One morning as I sat before the Lord, waiting to hear his voice, these words flowed into my mind: 'If you don't write down what I tell you, I won't give you any more.' Immediately I realised that I had not been journalling the words and pictures that he had been giving me, and I had forgotten some of them. I had been careless with that which was precious, and I needed to repent. I determined that, from that moment on, I would write down whatever I thought he was saying to me. In this way I would not lose anything, and I could test whether I was hearing him correctly.

I have found it hardest to hear the good things he speaks to me and often react by thinking, 'That's too wonderful. It couldn't possibly be for me! I must have got it wrong.' However, this was rooted in my lack of self-acceptance rather than in my inability to hear God's voice. As I learn to let his words flow spontaneously through me, I find myself surprised and delighted by their impact on my heart.

My natural reluctance to get it wrong for fear of deception or of dishonouring God can stop me hearing him at all. My rational analytical mind finds it hard to let my spirit speak at an intuitive level, but we all have to be prepared to make mistakes. No one ever learns to walk without falling over a great deal. So it is with hearing the Lord's voice. Only through practice and the wise advice of mature Christians will we learn to divide between his voice and the noise of our 'old nature'.

Soaked in the truth

As we learn to live under God's Word, and listen for his voice, we begin to perceive reality with the eyes of the Spirit. We will find that our society offends us more, yet moves us to greater compassion. The more we are rooted in truth, the less society's values will deceive us and the more objective we are enabled to be.

As his Word 'dwells richly in me' it enables me to live in greater purity and holiness. I am no longer able to excuse my sin so easily and yet I am more empowered to embrace the way of the Spirit. My behaviour changes because I learn to receive his life-imparting affirmation and encouragement. The old strongholds begin to crumble as the presence of his glorious truth brings freedom to my mind, heart and will.

> As we hear him we come into our full identity. We know who we are and who we were created to be and become. We pass from immaturity to maturity.[3]

There can be no true authenticity or maturity in our lives until we have come out from under the power of the old attitudes that are rooted in destructive and deceptive lies. It is the Word of God that will liberate us, feed us and cause us to change into the likeness of Christ.

> *Father God, I thank you that your Word brings life. Please show me where my thinking is darkened and where I have believed that which is not true about myself or about you. I choose today to identify, reject and renounce all destructive thinking and to look to you for your healing words. Please give me the grace to believe the words of blessing that you are going to speak to my mind and my heart. Amen.*

EXERCISES

1. Write down two aspects of the character of God that you need to be revealed more clearly (e.g. his holiness, his love, his power).

2. Write down two examples of your own destructive self-talk. Seek to identify where you first learned to think in this way.

3. Prayerfully choose a verse or passage that speaks directly to the four examples you have given above. Take time to go through the five steps to releasing the power of the Word. (You may need to express your emotions and do some forgiveness before you can receive God's Word into your heart.)

4. Spend time in listening prayer. Write down in your journal what the Lord shows you in response to these two questions:
   • Lord, what do you like about me?
   • Lord, how do you want me to change?

13

Created to Love

'If you had three years to save the world, what would you do?' asked the speaker as he prepared us to host a gathering of young adults. What a great question! I felt inspired and immediately began to think of an effective strategy. I would hold conferences, give high-profile television interviews, write a book or two, lead mass rallies . . . my imagination was creating big plans!

How would you answer the same question? If you had three years to save the world, what would your strategy be? Still in my daydream I was brought back to earth with a bump as the speaker continued: 'Jesus chose twelve men and spent time hanging out with them. He took twelve damaged and inade-quate guys and poured his time, love and attention into them. This was his central strategy for saving the world.'

I was stunned. I felt convicted of my own arrogance, independence and individualistic mindset, and I realised how far away from the heart of Jesus I really was. Jesus had a vision for the whole world but he began with just a few ordinary men. Relationships were at the core of his way of life; second only to his relationship with the Father, there was nothing that occupied his time and attention more than loving and nurturing his disciples.

Why was this so? Surely God could have come to earth and done so much more had he not been burdened and restricted by the struggles, doubts and weaknesses of his disciples?

The purpose of mankind is to love God and to love our neighbour, and it is only within the context of relationships that we are going to be able to express the reality of our faith. Jesus chose his disciples not just to meet his own need for friendship and love, but also in order that they might learn to live out the good news of the kingdom in an authentic way. This began as he shared his own life with that little band who walked the hills and villages of Palestine.

As they grew to know him and to believe his teaching, so they had to live it out among themselves. I am sure that Peter would often have felt that if only he could just be alone with Jesus he would have been so much more spiritual, patient and kind, but what a hard job it was loving the other eleven! After our mountain-top experiences with the Lord it is so much harder to get on with the work of really loving those around us, especially if they hurt us or irritate us!

> It is easier to be enthusiastic about Humanity with a capital H, than it is to love individual men and women, especially those who are uninteresting, exasperating, depraved or otherwise unattractive. Loving everybody in general may be an excuse for loving nobody in particular.[1]

There can be no genuine maturity in Christ that is not accompanied by loving, trusting and intimate relationships. If the goal of maturity is to love God with everything within us, then the litmus test for the reality of our maturity is: am I growing in my ability to love other people and to develop authentic relationships?

The vertical and the horizontal

In his first letter St John writes: 'We love because he first loved us. If anyone says, "I love God," yet hates his brother, he is a liar. For anyone who does not love his brother, whom he has seen, cannot love God, whom he has not seen. And he has given us this command: Whoever loves God must also love his brother' (1 John 4:19–21).

There is a powerful relationship between the way we relate vertically to God and horizontally to people. I cannot have a deep and profound relationship with God and at the same time withdraw from people and keep them at a distance. I cannot hate people and pretend that I still love God. The more I love God, the more that love will be expressed to those around me. Spiritual realities are always manifested in the physical realm. Intimate and authentic relationships with real people are a sign of an intimate and authentic relationship with a real God.

I woke up to this dynamic as God began to heal my own heart. As his love began to cleanse my heart of the old destructive emotions, and as I worked through my own pain and hurt, I found that I could love my wife, my children and my brothers and sisters in Christ in a new way and to a new depth. As I came to know my heart I could begin to share it more openly and so become more vulnerable and transparent. This enabled others to get closer to me and for me to get closer to them.

As this change was taking place I began to realise just how superficial my relationships had been before. I had sung worship songs about intimacy with God, I had read about it in books, and I thought I was being intimate with him, but in truth I wasn't. I was cut off from my own heart and my relationships were sadly lacking in depth and vulnerability.

Easily deceived

It is all too easy to cover up our lack of love with religious activity. Extraordinary as it may seem, St Paul teaches that it is possible to give generously to the poor, move in great spiritual power and die a martyr's death without any genuine love in our hearts (1 Corinthians 13:1–3). Religion is capable of great deception. We do those things that are expected of us by our particular church community, and then assume that because people are pleased with our actions, our hearts must be right before God himself. Our activity protects us from the realisation that our hearts are hard and cold and that our actions are not motivated by love at all, but by a strong desire to be applauded and accepted by our peers.

> It is difficult to express just how ingenious almost all people are in counterfeiting a love which they do not really possess. They deceive not only others but also themselves that they have a true love for those whom they not only treat with neglect, but also in fact reject.[2]

Very often our love grows cold without us even realising. We may still be reading our Bible, praying regularly and meeting with other believers, but we have withdrawn from being vulnerable and loving. When this happens we stop being lovers and become exploiters. Plans replace people, careers replace caring and activity replaces affection. In the name of God we manipulate others to fulfil our dreams and visions, or to meet our personal needs.

Authentic relationships

Authentic relationships are created by authentic people. When we hide behind masks we will not be authentic people, and our relationships will remain superficial and unfulfilling. To be authentic we must look to go deeper and become more real with one another. The Latin word *intimus* means 'innermost' and from this we derive our English word 'intimate'. Authentic relationships are intimate relationships in which we learn to express our innermost selves to one another. Intimacy is a big word and needs to be broken down into smaller, more manageable parts. To be intimate we need to be vulnerable, affectionate, accepting, caring and committed.

Being vulnerable

Sandra found relationships very hard to form. Growing up with parents who constantly criticised and ridiculed her, she had learned to withdraw behind her walls of self-protection. Her few friends found her hard to get to know and she found it hard to be open with them. Sandra had no real knowledge of what it meant to be vulnerable, she had never seen it within her family and felt so fragile that she was frightened to expose herself to more rejection.

At university Sandra fell in with a group of Christians who were seeking to be vulnerable and transparent with one another. They were all learning to take off their masks and be honest. Slowly Sandra began to share herself with her friends. Encouraged by their acceptance of her she began to open like a flower bud, and in the safety of their love and commitment she began to grow and flourish.

So often we are like billiard balls that bounce off one another with no depth of contact. 'How are you?' we ask, not really wanting to know. 'I'm fine,' we reply, not really wanting to tell.

By not sharing our pain, our fears or our struggles with sin, we are able to create an atmosphere of spiritual unreality.

Having created it, everyone begins to conform to the prevailing culture and perpetuate the myth of spiritual success. Outwardly all is fine but inwardly we are hurt, fearful, lonely and anxious. We become inauthentic as the gap between our public and private lives widens. The prevailing atmosphere of 'niceness' suppresses true relationships. When we stop playing games with one another and dare to speak the truth courageously, we become people who have learned to meet at the foot of the cross. There, we broken, hurting and wounded people renounce our superficiality and confess our needs to one another. True intimacy begins to take place and true love begins to flow:

> True fellowship which binds our hearts together in love begins when we meet at the point of weakness. When I am willing to be open to you about my own personal needs, risking your shock and rejection, and when I am willing for you to be equally open with me, loving you with unjudging friendship, we find ourselves both at the foot of the cross, where there is level ground at the place of God's healing grace.[3]

Jesus was deeply vulnerable and transparent. In the Garden of Gethsemane he confessed his need of help to his disciples and admitted his deep pain to them. 'My soul is full of sorrow even to the point of death.' In effect Jesus was saying, 'I feel like dying, this hurts so much. Please pray with me.' How often are we as honest as Jesus? As we learn to 'put off falsehood and speak truthfully to our neighbour' (Ephesians 4:25) it will involve sharing our hopes and fears, our pain and our joys, our failures and our triumphs. We will break the illusion of spiritual invincibility and renounce our independent self-sufficiency. In this way we learn to become accountable to one another. We give one another permission to speak honestly into each other's lives, and freely allow others to call us to account for the way we live. This is part of what it means to become inter-dependent and die to our self-sufficient and independent tendencies.

Jimmy Swaggart, the tele-evangelist whose fall into sexual immorality was the focus of media attention in the late 1980s, wrote these words shortly before his demise: 'I have always taken great pride in my spiritual strength. I have believed that in my relationship with God, if he promised me something I could have it. I can't recall, in all my life, ever going to anybody and asking them for help.'[4] One can only wonder whether his fall into sexual immorality might have been avoided if he had dared share his personal struggles with one or two close friends.

John Wesley taught his converts to value fellowship and to become accountable to one another. He established converts in small cell groups for mutual care and discipling, and every time they met they would ask one another these five questions:

1. What sins have you committed since our last meeting?
2. What temptations have you met with?
3. How were you delivered?
4. What have you thought, said or done of which you doubt whether it be sin or not?
5. Have you nothing you desire to keep secret?

Wesley knew that if our walk with Christ is to be real, and if we are to be kept from self-deception, then we have to learn to be transparent and vulnerable with one another.

Being affectionate

Godly affection is released through the presence of the Holy Spirit within our hearts. Love is the first fruit of the Spirit to be mentioned in Galatians 5:22, and in 1 Peter 4:8 we are urged to 'love each other deeply'. To love deeply must involve our emotions. As a young Christian I was taught that I did not need to feel love in order to express love. To a certain extent this is true because agape is more than a feeling, but I must never be content to love solely out of duty. Instead I must seek God for a deep heartfelt love, even for my enemies. To pursue maturity means to work towards a love in which our emotions reflect the emotions of the Spirit. God so loved the world – and so must we.

When men and women are cut off from their own emotions or are controlled by their feelings, they will fail to consistently impart the love of God to others. When emotions are frozen or destructive feelings pour out of the heart, we need to recognise that we are still in need of repentance and healing. The more our love tanks are filled with God's love, the more we will be moved by God's emotions. Just as a river fills the buckets of a waterwheel which then pours water upon dry ground, so our hearts will pour out God's love to the extent that we have first received it. We cannot give away what we have not first received.

When deep affections of compassion and mercy flow from within us, people feel the love imparted more than the words or actions can convey. When there is no true love from the heart, then our words and actions can seem hollow and patronising.

We cannot fulfil the commandment to love in our own strength. True maturity recognises this bankruptcy and the deceitfulness of our own hearts, and runs to the cross for forgiveness and a fresh baptism of divine love.

Being accepting

To create intimacy we must learn to accept one another without criticism, judgment or comparison. 'Accept one another, then, just as Christ accepted you' (Romans 15:7). When God accepted you, he accepted you as you were with all your faults and weaknesses and with all your strengths and talents. God's acceptance is an unconditional acceptance.

When I fail to accept myself, I will fail to accept others. If I compare, analyse and judge myself, then I will do the same to others. Because Jesus was at ease with himself and never sought to live up to the expectations of others, he was able to accept each person for who they were. There is no record of him ever having compared his disciples to one another. He never said to Peter, 'If only you could be a little more spiritual like John.' Nor did he ever say to John, 'Stop being so serious, John. Get a life! Try and be a bit more spontaneous like Peter!'

It was this loving acceptance that enabled Jesus to make the prostitutes and thieves feel quite at home in his company. He loved them and accepted them for who they were. Accepting one another does not mean we condone sinful behaviour. Instead we look past the sin and see the hurting and wounded person behind the behaviour. Knowing what it is to be accepted and forgiven ourselves, we do not judge or condemn others. We are only able to speak the truth in love if there is genuine love and compassion in our hearts. Self-righteousness and compassion cannot live together.

Richard Griffiths was in England when the news reached that Ken Andrews, an old friend from his church in the States, had been convicted of procuring teenage boys for sex. Richard and Ken had been good friends and had shared much together, but hearing this news made Richard sick to the pit of his

stomach. He felt betrayed, angry and disgusted at Ken's behaviour. But in the midst of all these emotions God spoke to
Richard and told him to go and visit Ken in jail. This was very
difficult for him to hear and even harder for him to do, but
finally, after quite a battle, Richard gave in, and on his next
visit to America he went to see Ken.

When they met face to face God had done such a work in
Richard's heart that he was able to accept Ken as he was, and
to tell him that, despite everything, God still loved him and he
also still loved him. In the presence of such acceptance Ken
broke down in tears and wept. His church had utterly rejected
him and he had lost his wife and children, but as they spoke
the presence of God filled the room and touched Ken's heart
deeply.

Acceptance is the cornerstone of intimacy. We will never
dare to reveal our brokenness and sin to one another if a judgmental spirit is present. When I accept you for who God made
you to be and as you accept me also, then we are both able to
be ourselves. In the presence of true acceptance the masks
come down and we find that we are loved and valued just as
we are.

Being caring

In *The Road Less Travelled* Scott Peck describes how love
must focus on the needs of the other person:

> The principal form that the work of love takes is attention. When
> we love another we give him or her our attention. When we attend
> to someone we are caring for that person.[5]

We will never truly love one another while we are still bound
up in our own needs and desires. At the beginning of the book
I told the story of Narcissus, who fell in love with his own

reflection and finally drowned while trying to kiss his own reflection. We are all prone to narcissistic tendencies. It is part of our continual struggle to break out of the sin of self-preoccupation and to centre our hearts and minds on God and those around us.

A mother was telling her six-year-old about the golden rule. 'Always remember that we are here to love others.' The child mulled this over for a moment or two and then replied, 'Well, what are the others here for?'

I relate very easily to that six-year-old. I find it much easier to expect others to remember my needs, to forgive my faults and to care for my wounds. Taking my eyes off myself is like dragging metal away from a magnet. It can be done, but only with difficulty. To walk the way of love means to focus our attention on the needs of others. This is another way of saying that we are called to have servant hearts that delight in caring for one another's needs. The spiritual discipline of loving service is one of the ways in which we put to death our self-centred narcissism. Just as Jesus 'did not come to be served, but to serve' (Matthew 20:28) so we too are called to follow his example. True maturity is willing to serve without looking for reward. It is a free gift given out of the overflow of hearts that have been filled with God's love. Mature service is a response to the leading of the Spirit and is not remotely co-dependent or self-seeking.

In relationships we quickly find that we prefer to take, to own and to possess one another. We look to others to meet our needs before we will meet theirs. The way of the Spirit is to lead us into self-sacrifice. By giving to and serving one another we find that we are being healed and learning to live in the love of God.

Jackie Pullinger worked in the Walled City in Hong Kong.

With its narrow streets, open sewers, brothels and drug dens it was a place of deep darkness. Every day Jackie would pass an old lady who had been a prostitute for sixty years. One day she and Jackie talked about Jesus and the old lady was saved.

This lady had been a heroin addict for a long time, and over the years she had used up all the veins in her arms and legs. Through prayer and the power of the Holy Spirit she came off drugs and moved in to live with Jackie. Bit by bit she began to recover from sixty years of abuse, but before too long she entered the 'bad temper' phase. She would demand that God should help her more and forget how wonderful it was of him to save her in the first place. Every meeting that she came to she asked for healing prayer. This went on for some time, until Jackie began to ask, 'God, when is this going to stop? How long must we go on ministering to her?' It went on for seven years with the old lady getting prayed for at every meeting.

One day they went to help out at another old people's home, and the old lady came back quite distressed. 'It's awful!' she cried. 'People don't love them. We've got so much more than they have. People don't wash them in their beds. People don't tell them about Jesus.' From that day on she went to the old people's home to wash their hair and their clothes and to tell them about Jesus, and from that day on she began to be fully healed. Jackie explained: 'It was when she saw there were others who were as poor as she had been, and when she gave up her right to her ministry in favour of theirs, that she was healed.' On 25 July 1992 she was married to a seventy-five-year-old man named Little Wa.

To serve one another is a sign of maturity and also the path to maturity and wholeness. It breaks our self-preoccupation and releases into our lives the blessing of Jesus: 'Now that I, your Lord and Teacher, have washed your feet, you also should wash one another's feet . . . now that you know these things you will be blessed if you do them' (John 13:14, 17).

Being committed

As soon as we enter any relationship or belong to any community we will quickly realise that it is imperfect. We hurt one another because we are imperfect and self-centred creatures. As God's children we are saved, but we have not yet been made perfect. If we are still living out of a self-focused and self-centred attitude, then when the first experiences of rejection or disappointment come we will be tempted to stop being open and vulnerable. We need to come to terms with the fact that there are no perfect people, no perfect relationships and no perfect churches. Once we have accepted this fact we can begin to love and be loved where God has put us.

> Just as surely as God desires to lead us to a knowledge of genuine Christian fellowship, so surely we must be overwhelmed by a great general disillusionment with others, with Christians, and, if we are fortunate, with ourselves . . . The sooner this shock of disillusionment comes to an individual and to a community the better for both . . . When the morning mists of dreams vanish, then dawns the bright day of Christian fellowship.[6]

We must come to terms with our own brokenness and that of the people around us. If we will choose to work at our relationships and if we will determine to live a life of forgiveness, trust and honesty, then true intimacy and true community become a real possibility.

Our society is deeply influenced by the spirit of consumerism. We expect to be served just what we want and just when we want it, and if we can't find what we are looking for we move on to the next person, the next church or the next community. Consumerism is about taking, but intimacy is about committed giving. The depth of our commitment to know and be known reveals the reality of the love that is in our hearts for the other person. It was Christ's utter commitment to us that led to his death. We too must learn to commit ourselves to one another in a way that pushes us out of our comfort zones. Without serious commitment our relationships will for ever remain shallow and superficial.

The call to community

As we persevere towards sharing genuinely authentic and intimate relationships with a few people, we will be sowing the seeds for a genuinely Christ-centred community. God's design for the church is that it should be a community in which hurting, broken and needy people (in other words, all of us!) are enabled to bare their wounds and find healing and love.

So far this book has been primarily individualistic, focusing on personal growth to maturity, but an individual can only change within the context of relationships. We have looked at Paul's prayer in Ephesians 3 in relation to the filling of our personal love tanks, and I believe that is a right and appropriate use of the passage, but note what it says in verses 17 and 18 (italics mine): 'And I pray that you, being rooted and established in love, may have power, *together with all the saints*, to grasp how wide and long and high and deep is the love of Christ.'

We learn to know this love of Christ together. As we care for one another and pursue deeper and more intimate relationships, then we will experience the presence of the love of God among us in extraordinary ways. God is looking to dwell in manifest presence among a people who are seeking to love him and are committed to loving one another.

Where community begins

Community begins with me. As I choose to invest myself in a few intimate relationships and to live a life of service, then I will be creating community. Stuck in narcissistic attitudes, demanding that my needs be met, I will be destroying community. There are times to give and times to receive within any relationship or community, but our primary motivation must be to serve others first as an expression of our love for God.

Jesus developed intimate relationships with only a few people. Peter, James and John, and Mary, Martha and Lazarus are those with whom he appears to have shared himself most fully. In each of our lives we have hundreds, maybe thousands, of relationships, but we can't be intimate with everyone. There is not the time and we do not have sufficient emotional energy. We need to pray that God would show us who to be intimate with. Generally we will need to go deeper with the people we already know, though God may bring new people into our lives. Remember, there are no perfect relationships and no perfect people. Begin with the imperfect people you already know!

> In our culture, relationships are disposable like cans and containers. You use them and then you throw them away. With Jesus it is an eternal relationship. The apostolic community followed that relationship of Jesus with the Twelve. I urge you to think about that. Find a small group of sisters or brothers for whom you feel a responsibility and to whom you are accountable. Meet with them regularly and you'll be amazed at how the influence of that little group will spread everywhere.[7]

When we think about the abolition of slavery, the name William Wilberforce quickly springs to mind. It took Wilberforce from 1791 to 1833 to bring it about, but he was only able to persevere in the face of great opposition because he had developed strong and supportive relationships with a group of friends who came to be known as the Clapham Sect. Billy Graham has also consistently met with the same group of friends for forty-seven years. These high-profile public ministries have their roots in deep personal friendships.

Are you seeking to develop authentic and intimate relationships with a few people? It seems that so many believers feel isolated and alone despite their churches, their home groups and even their friends. I urge you to take some initiative and begin to pray and to seek to commit yourself to a few relationships where you can begin to allow one another to take off the masks, and where you can minister to one another the unconditional and healing love of God.

Giving it all away

There are no fish in Israel's Dead Sea because the water is too saturated with salt for them to survive. Even though fresh water flows into it every day, the Dead Sea has no outflow and so the heat of the sun evaporates the water, leaving only its salty deposit. Just a few miles north, the Sea of Galilee is teeming with life because the Jordan river flows into it and then out again on its way south. Unless we are giving away the life that Christ has given to us, we too will become stagnant. It is as we choose to give that we will then receive fresh fillings of the love of God: 'Give, and it will be given to you. A good measure, pressed down, shaken together and running over will be poured into your lap. For with the measure you use, it will be measured to you' (Luke 6:38).

As we look away from ourselves and cry out to God to enlarge our capacity to love, he will pour his love into our hearts in order that we might give it away to others. As we are healed and restored and grow to maturity, we are also commissioned to become wounded healers in a broken world.

Healthy people make healthy relationships, which create healthy communities that can share the good news of the love of God with real integrity. In order to become the people that God has made us to be, we must determine to grow in our capacity to give and receive love, and in so doing we will fulfil the very purpose for which we were created. It is as we are loved, and as we love, that the real self is renewed in the image of God.

Father God, I ask you to reveal to me the true state of my heart. Please show me where my love has grown cold, and where I have supplanted the call to authentic love with activity and empty words. I choose today to learn again what it means to live a life of love, and I invite you to remove all the hindrances within my own heart. Thank you for your endless patience and determined grace to bring me to maturity and to cause the real me to stand up. Amen.

EXERCISES

1. To what degree have you sought to make love the primary purpose in your life?

   What other things (e.g. success, activity, power, pleasure) are you tempted to replace it with?

2. Number each of the different aspects of intimacy in descending order to reflect which you find the easiest and which the hardest:

- Vulnerability
- Accountability
- Affection
- Acceptance
- Caring
- Commitment

In what ways could you develop each of these in your life?

3. Using Figure 11, decide who are the people with whom you share different levels of intimacy.
   A = spouse, children
   B = intimate friends
   C = close friends
   D = acquaintances

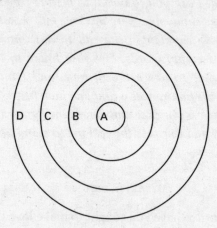

Figure 11 – Levels of intimacy

Spend time in prayer asking the Lord to deepen existing friendships and to bring people into your life who can fill any obvious gaps revealed above.

Conclusion

There is a certain type of Chinese bamboo that grows in a rather unique way. In the first year that it is planted, the farmer feeds it and waters it but he sees no growth at all. In the second year the farmer continues to feed it and water it, but still he sees no signs of the shoots. This goes on through the third and fourth years, but in the fifth year, in the right season, the bamboo grows to thirty feet within five days. It may have taken a while, but all the farmer's hard work and patience is fully rewarded. Let me ask you a question: did that bamboo grow to thirty feet in five days or five years?

So often we look for instant change and immediate maturity, but in reality it takes time for our real selves to emerge from the graveclothes of the old nature. As we set our eyes on the prize of knowing Christ and being made like him, and as we invest our lives into the four critical areas that this book has covered, then we will see change that is real and lasting. The growth to maturity does not come without a fight and Satan will use every weapon he has to stop you. In particular he will seek to convince you that you aren't changing and that all your time and effort will be wasted. In Galatians 6:7–9,

Paul responds to this temptation, which is common to all believers:

> Do not be deceived; God cannot be mocked. A man reaps what he sows. The one who sows to please his sinful nature, from that nature will reap destruction; the one who sows to please the Spirit, from the Spirit will reap eternal life. Let us not become weary in doing good, for at the proper time we will reap a harvest if we do not give up.

Let me remind you at the close of this book that the principle that God has established is one of sowing and reaping, not reaping and sowing! You have to invest of yourself into the ways of God before you will see your harvest. But your harvest of life will surely come as you keep on growing in your understanding of God's amazing grace, facing up to and working through your emotional brokenness, renouncing the false comforts that the world offers, and above all embracing the way of the Spirit. God cannot be mocked; his eternal principles cannot be overturned. Those who sow to the Spirit will reap eternal life, now and in the world to come – if we don't give up!

May the real you, suffused with the presence of Christ himself in every aspect of your being, shine forth to the honour and glory of God the Father. Amen.

Notes

Chapter 1 – Embracing the Real Self

1. W. E. Vine, *Vine's Complete Expository Dictionary of Old and New Testament Words*, Thomas Nelson 1984, p. 559.
2. Leanne Payne, *The Real Presence*, Kingsway 1989, p. 160.
3. C. S. Lewis, *The Great Divorce*, Centenary Press 1945, p. 159.
4. Briar Whitehead, *Craving for Love*, Monarch 1993, p. 77.
5. *Die Annahme seiner selbst ed.* Werkbandverlag 1969, pp. 14, 16. Quoted in Walter Trobisch, *Love Yourself: Self-Acceptance and Depression*, InterVarsity Press 1976, p. 9.
6. Margery Williams, *The Velveteen Rabbit*, William Heinemann 1983, p. 4.

Chapter 2 – The Wonderful Riches of His Grace

1. W. E. Vine, *Vine's Complete Expository Dictionary of Old and New Testament Words*, p. 531.
2. C. S. Lewis, *Mere Christianity*, Fount 1955, p. 136.

Chapter 3 – Will the Real Me Please Stand Up

1. Leanne Payne, *The Real Presence*, p. 15.
2. Watchman Nee, *The Spiritual Man*, Christian Fellowship Publishers 1968, p. 66.
3. Dr and Mrs Howard Taylor, *The Biography of James Hudson Taylor*, Hodder & Stoughton 1965, p. 308.

Chapter 4 – Exposing the Strongholds

1. I have adapted the principles found in Josh McDowell's *His Image, My Image*, Scripture Press 1984, p. 100.
2. Victor Frankl, *Man's Search for Meaning*, Hodder & Stoughton 1962.

Chapter 5 – Foundations for Real Change

1. Josh McDowell, *His Image, My Image*, p. 34.
2. Dr Ross Campbell, *How to Really Love Your Child*, Scripture Press 1977, p. 39.
3. *Reader's Digest* article 'The Sense that Shapes our Future', January 1992. As quoted in *How to Really Love Your Child*, p. 56.
4. Peter Dainty, *The Love of a King*, Oxford Bookworms 1989, p. 3.

Chapter 7 – The Healing Power of Christ

1. Mario Bergner, *Setting Love in Order*, Baker Books 1995.

Chapter 8 – Kicking the Habit

1. Jeffrey Satinover, *Homosexuality and the Politics of Truth*, Hamewith Books 1996, p. 130.

2. Briar Whitehead, *Craving for Love*, p. 33.
3. Jeffrey Satinover, *Homosexuality and the Politics of Truth*, p. 147.
4. R. Hemfelt, F. Minirth, P. Meier, *Love is a Choice*, Monarch Books 1990, p. 78.

Chapter 9 – Easing the Pain

1. Lori Rentzel, *Emotional Dependency*, InterVarsity Press 1991, p. 8.
2. M. Scott Peck, *The Road Less Travelled*, Arrow 1978, p. 112.
3. *The California Lawyer* (November 1989), as quoted in Briar Whitehead, *Craving for Love*, p. 56.
4. J. A. Walter, *A Long Way from Home*, Paternoster Press 1979, p. 28.

Chapter 10 – Hungry for Love

1. *Leadership* 9, 'How common is pastoral indiscretion?', Winter 1988, p. 12.
2. Richard Foster, *Money, Sex and Power*, Hodder & Stoughton 1985, p. 92.
3. C. S. Lewis, *Mere Christianity*, Fount 1955, p. 86.
4. Leanne Payne, *The Healing Presence*, Kingsway 1990, p. 123.

Chapter 11 – Seeking the Face of God

1. Benny Hinn, *Good Morning, Holy Spirit*, Word Books 1990, p. 56.
2. 'A Life in the Day of Desmond Tutu', *Sunday Times Magazine*, 16 October 1994.

3. Julian of Norwich, *Revelations of Divine Love*, Penguin Classics 1966, p. 71.

4. Leanne Payne, *The Healing Presence*, p. 24.

Chapter 12 – Truth that Sets Us Free

1. Francis Frangipane, *The Three Battlegrounds*, Advancing Church Publications 1989, p. 83.

2. A. W. Tozer, *The Knowledge of the Holy*, Kingsway 1989.

3. Leanne Payne, *Listening Prayer*, Kingsway 1994, p. 128.

Chapter 13 – Created to Love

1. C. S. Lewis.

2. John Calvin quoted in C. E. B. Cranfield, *Romans*, T. & T. Clark 1985, p. 310.

3. David Watson, *Discipleship*, Hodder & Stoughton 1981, p. 51.

4. Jimmy Swaggart, 'The Lord of the Breaking Through' in *The Evangelist*, March 1988, p. 7. Quoted in C. Peter Wagner, *Prayer Shield*, Monarch 1992, p. 97.

5. M. Scott Peck. *The Road Less Travelled*, Arrow 1978, p. 128.

6. Dietrich Bonhoeffer, *Life Together*, SCM Press 1954, p. 15.

7. Dan Quayle speaking at the National Prayer Breakfast in Washington DC, 1989 – an annual gathering of American leaders for prayer in the name of Christ, hosted by the President.